GROWTH AND DEVELOPMENT

OTHER TITLES IN THIS SERIES:

Bad Behaviour, Tantrums and Tempers (Dr John Pearce)
Families and Friends (Dr John Pearce)
Food: Too Faddy, Too Fat (Dr John Pearce)
Good Habits, Bad Habits (Dr John Pearce)
Successful Potty Training (Heather Welford)
Teach Your Baby to Sleep through the Night
(Charles E. Schaefer and Michael R. Petronko)
Worries and Fears (Dr John Pearce)
You Can Teach Your Child about Numbers (Adrienne Katz)
You Can Teach Your Child to Read (Adrienne Katz)

Dr John Pearce

GROWTH AND DEVELOPMENT

Thorsons
An Imprint of HarperCollins*Publishers*

Thorsons
An Imprint of HarperCollins*Publishers*
77-85 Fulham Palace Road,
Hammersmith, London W6 8JB
1160 Battery Street,
San Francisco, California 94111-1213

Published by Thorsons 1994
1 3 5 7 9 10 8 6 4 2

A catalogue record for this book
is available from the British Library

ISBN 0 7225 1724 6

Typeset by Harper Phototypesetters Limited
Northampton, England
Printed and bound in Great Britain by
HarperCollinsManufacturing Glasgow

To Mary

Contents

• • • • •

Introduction

· · · · ·

'Is my child healthy?' This is the first question that parents ask, even before their child is born. But as soon as it is clear that the child is healthy and well, the next question comes along - 'Is my child developing properly?' This question is much more difficult to answer with a clear yes or no and, not surprisingly, concern about each developmental stage continues to be one of the main preoccupations for parents as their children grow older.

The aim of this book is to help parents to understand children's development in a general way. I have covered a wider range of areas of development than is usual in a parent guidebook. I have also covered what is considered 'normal' development in some detail because it is only by knowing what is considered normal that you will be able to recognize any developmental delay or problems in your child.

By reading this book it should be possible for you to have a good idea about how your child is progressing through the various stages of development. You will also be able to learn something about the process of development from birth to adolescence.

One of the most complicated things about development is that there is so much individual variation. This is what confuses parents and often makes it difficult to give a straight answer to questions about development. Differences in the stages of development can appear to be very marked in younger children while at the same time being well within what is considered the normal range.

At the same time it is possible for individual children to have a range of skills, some of which are advanced and others that are delayed. A good example of this is the child who is generally developing well but continues to wet the bed at a much older age than normal, or the child who has great difficulty in learning to read in spite of developing well in all other ways.

In addition to details about the main stages of development you will find information on areas of 'Specific Developmental Delay', such as reading problems or bedwetting, where general development is progressing satisfactorily but one or more specific skills are delayed in relation to the rest of the child's development.

Between 10 and 20 per cent of all children experience a significant degree of Specific Developmental Delay. The following conditions are examples of this special and often misunderstood developmental disorder:

- communication problems after two years old
- clumsiness after three years old
- soiling after four years old
- wetting day and/or night after five years old
- reading difficulties after seven years old.

It can be difficult to understand what is happening if an apparently normal child doesn't reach a developmental milestone at the expected time. Considerable confusion and distress can occur as a result of delayed development, especially if your child appears normal in other ways.

It isn't unusual for parents to be the first to realize that something is wrong with their child's development, then to have teachers and others reassure them, only to find that they (the parents) were right all along. If you are one of these parents, you should find that this book offers an explanation for what is happening with your child and what you can do to help. Also how to help others to understand your child and his or her particular needs.

More than 20 children in every 1000 are born with a general delay in development that is so severe that all aspects of development are affected, resulting in learning difficulty. About 10 per cent of all children have a specific developmental difficulty where only one or two aspects of development are affected. These two groups of children put an extra responsibility on their parents.

You might ask, 'Why do parents need to read a book on child development? Surely there is nothing that can be done to change the way a child develops?' To some extent this is certainly true, but understanding what to expect can reduce the worry about what may seem to be abnormal development, and appropriate training can speed up lagging development.

Over the past few years there have been great advances in the understanding of how development progresses and what can be done to help it to progress. It is no longer necessary just to hope that your child will grow up without problems of development.

Unfortunately, the complete information on development isn't easily available to the general public, mostly because research is published in so many different scientific journals. Keeping up to date with current findings is therefore difficult for parents. In writing this book I have used the best of the research findings and I have also used all the guidelines myself in my work with children and families, so I can confidently recommend them to you.

You may be surprised to find that most, if not all of the suggestions that I make sound like basic common sense. This should reassure you, but many busy parents find that so-called 'common sense' is not that easy to come by. In any case, experts don't always agree. At least you will know that the approaches outlined in this book are based on many years of practical experience, helping children to develop and teaching parents how to understand what developmental problems they can do something about.

I would like you to feel that I am talking directly to you as you read through this book. You can 'talk' back to me if you don't agree with what I have said or if you don't understand. Then read on and it should become clear why I have taken a certain line rather than any other. Don't hold back from having an argument with me in your head or asking someone else what he or she thinks. In this way you will become much clearer about what you believe yourself.

Childcare is not so much about right and wrong, but more about finding the best compromise between the various demands of family life. For this reason it is impossible to 'get it right' all the time and this often leads to feelings of guilt. In fact, a normal part of being a parent is feeling guilty about not always doing the right thing for your child! These feelings can be particularly strong for parents with a child whose development seems to be hampered in some way.

If you are unsure about your own ideas but have some reservations about what I have written, I would like you to follow my suggestions as closely as possible, in spite of any reservations you might have. I have been very careful to give guidelines and advice only where I am confident that it is safe, reasonable and effective. If you have followed the guidelines carefully and they have still not worked, please don't immediately think that I have got it all wrong. It is much more likely that you haven't been sticking closely enough to what I have said. So read the book again, have another go ... and don't give up!

It is the love you have for your child that makes being a parent so fulfilling and joyful. But it is this same bond of affection that makes it so painful and distressing when things go wrong. Having a child with developmental problems can make a parent's feelings of love change to frightening feelings of confusion and sometimes rejection. Many parents will find themselves thinking 'why me?' Fortunately it isn't necessary to love your child all the time in order to be a reasonable parent. But basic care and protection are vital.

I hope that there is something of interest for everyone, even if you have no children. You might even find out something about your own development. After all, we continue developing even as adults.

1

. . . . .

Stages and Ages of Development

THE EARLY YEARS

It is difficult for parents to avoid worrying about how their child is developing and whether or not all is going according to plan. At the same time many parents hope that their child may be advanced in development - perhaps even a genius! Comparisons are made with other children and it can easily become rather like a competition for who has the most rapidly developing child.

In spite of this competitive urge, most parents would agree that they want nothing more for their children than that they should fulfil their potential and be happy - neither of which is related to being very bright. Most parents would agree that it is more important to them that their child grows up to be kind, generous and gentle rather than being a 'clever clogs'.

Nevertheless it is impossible not to be fascinated by children's development. It is so exciting when each new stage is reached and children as well as parents gain a great deal of satisfaction when progress is made.

It is a mistake to put too much emphasis on when a particular stage has been reached. There is a wide range of normal variation. So don't get too hung up on what stage your child has reached, unless you feel that his or her progress is very much out of step with other children.

So much development occurs during the early years of life that I have made detailed lists of the main developmental stages that are passed through during this period. With these lists you can work out how your child is progressing. However, these developmental stages should only be used as *general* guidelines. It would be quite unusual for any child to have gained all the skills listed at the expected time. Many children are behind with one or two areas of development. So don't panic if this is the case with your child. Remember that there is a wide variation in the range of normal development in young children and that boys generally develop more slowly than girls.

During the first few months it can be extremely difficult to tell if a child's development is progressing normally because so many changes happen so quickly. Note how many more developmental stages are being reached in the early months compared with, say, in the year before your child starts school.

As time goes on, any delay in development will become more obvious. Even at five years old it may not be at all clear whether or not a child is developing at the expected rate. However, it is often the case that by this stage many parents will have formed a general impression that something is not quite right with their child's development - often before the experts are able to confirm this.

THE FIRST FOUR WEEKS

Here are some of the main physical characteristics of the average new-born baby:

- respiratory rate: 30-50 breaths per minute
- pulse rate: 120-150 heartbeats per minute
- weight: 2.8-3.75 kg/6-8.25 lb (boys are slightly heavier than girls)
- length: 45-54 cm/18-21 inches
- head circumference: 32-37 cm/13-15 inches
- visual acuity: 20/100 (normal = 20/20)
- temperature: 35.5 - 37°C/95.5-98.6°F

At birth there is a whole range of automatic reflexes such as those for sucking and swallowing, coughing, blinking and emptying the bowels and bladder. Premature or developmentally delayed babies may not have all the normal reflexes and experts will check the many different reflexes to assess the degree of delay in development. There are two interesting reflexes that you can look for: the grasp reflex, where the baby will hold anything placed in the hand, and the stepping reflex, where walking movements are made if the baby is held with the feet just touching a flat surface.

Here are some of the things that a new-born baby can do in the first month of life:

- sees outlines and shapes best at about 30 cm/12 inches
- turns head from side to side
- follows a slowly moving object through 180 degrees
- prefers mother's voice to a stranger's
- hears, tastes and smells almost as well as an adult
- moves to familiar sounds
- makes sounds other than crying
- enjoys being picked up and cuddled
- responds differently to different individuals
- indicates need for a nappy change and feeding time
- enjoys bathing in warm water and being fussed over
- sleeps as long as five to seven hours

ONE TO FOUR MONTHS

- grows at about 2.5 cm/1 inch per month
- weighs about 3.5-7 kg/8-16 lb (0.25-0.5 kg/0.5-1 lb per week)
- respiratory rate: 30-40 breaths per minute
- pulse rate: 120-150 beats per minute
- head circumference increasing by 2 cm/0.75 in during the first two months and then by 1.5 cm/0.8 in until four months
- stepping reflex disappears

- holds hands open or semi-open
- raises head when lying on tummy
- reaches for objects
- puts hands together
- rolls from front to back and sits supported by the end of this period
- recognizes colour and familiar objects
- puts objects in the mouth
- turns head towards sound and connects sounds and rhythms
- co-ordinates vision, voice and movements
- smiles sociably and later on laughs out loud
- uses eyes and sounds to keep others' attention
- eyes focus together

FOUR TO EIGHT MONTHS

- grows at 1.3 cm/0.5 inch per month
- doubles original birth weight, gaining at 0.45 kg/1 lb per month
- head circumference increases by 1 cm/0.4 inch per month from four to six months and 0.5 cm/0.25 inch from six to eight months
- teeth begin to appear
- mouthing objects, dribbling and chewing increase
- true eye colour established
- uses finger and thumb together (pincer grasp)
- transfers objects from one hand to the other
- holds own bottle
- sits without support
- lifts head when lying on back
- pulls into crawling position
- locates familiar sounds
- focuses eyes on small objects
- explores own body and surroundings
- plays with toys
- imitates actions of others – such as waving 'bye-bye'

- searches for hidden toy (object permanence)
- enjoys banging things together
- responds to own name
- makes wide range of sounds, including all vowels
- babbles and imitates sounds
- responds to simple requests
- distinguishes between different people
- deliberately seeks attention
- puts arms out to be picked up
- plays peek-a-boo games
- begins to eat solid food
- sleeps 11 to 13 hours at night
- has one to three naps during the day

EIGHT MONTHS TO ONE YEAR

- grows at 1.3 cm/0.5 inch per month and is one and a half times the length at birth by the first birthday
- birthweight is almost tripled by first birthday
- head circumference and chest circumference are equal
- has about 10 teeth
- can focus on objects up to 6 m/20 ft away
- able to stack objects
- pulls to standing and walks if hands are held
- crawls up and down stairs
- throws toys down and looks for them
- plays pretend games
- nods and shakes head
- makes language-like sounds to initiate social interaction
- says 'dada' – usually first – and then 'mama'
- responds to name
- enjoys rhymes and songs
- shows definite fear of strangers
- starts to be assertive

- understands the meaning of 'no'
- frequently become attached to a comforter
- enjoys taking shoes, socks and wet nappies off
- plays alone for up to 15 minutes
- drinks from a cup
- finger feeds and throws food around
- stands alone
- understands the use of everyday objects

ONE YEAR TO 18 MONTHS

- rate of growth begins to slow down - 6-8 cm/2.5-3 inches per year
- gains weight at 0.1-0.2 kg/3.5-7 oz per month
- respiratory rate: 24-30 breaths per minute at rest
- pulse rate: 80-120 beats per minute at rest
- head circumference increases by 1.3 cm/0.5 inches every six months
- chest circumference larger than head circumference
- fontanelle (soft spot on top of head) closes
- begins to walk alone, but often falls
- crawls backwards downstairs
- scribbles
- builds a tower of two to four bricks
- looks at pictures and turns pages of a book
- carries toys around
- passes objects from one hand to another
- can hold spoon but makes a mess
- knows names of everyday objects
- uses five to 50 words
- uses gesture to communicate needs (e.g. pointing)
- knows which objects go together (e.g. cup and saucer)
- obeys simple instructions
- can point to three parts of the body

- can make two-word phrases
- only about 25 per cent of speech can be understood
- imitates what adults do
- becomes more self-assertive and resistive
- recognizes self in a mirror
- becomes more friendly and curious
- enjoys songs and being read to

18 MONTHS TO TWO YEARS

- height: about 81-84 cm/32-33 inches (almost half adult height)
- weight: about 11-15 kg/24-33 lb (four times birth weight)
- head circumference increases by 1.3 cm/0.5 inches within six months
- has about 20 teeth
- chews food and feeds self with some mess
- runs and seldom falls
- climbs stairs one step at a time
- walks backwards
- throws a ball
- builds a tower of four to six bricks
- climbs up on a chair and sits on it
- bends down without falling over
- uses feet to move a wheeled toy along
- opens doors
- searches actively for a hidden toy
- anticipates problems (e.g. something falling over)
- repeats words that others have used
- uses 50-300 words
- uses two- to three-word phrases
- asks 'what' and 'why' questions
- speech is about 60 per cent understandable
- refers to self as 'me'
- shows deliberate defiance and affection

- alternates between independence and dependence
- possessive with toys, says 'mine'
- enjoys imaginary games
- watches other children play, seldom joins in
- undresses but needs help with dressing
- becoming toilet-trained (bowels usually first)
- plays in parallel with other children

THE THIRD YEAR TO AGE FOUR

- grows about 5–8 cm/2–3 inches per year (twice birth length at three years).
- At three years old the child's eventual height can be worked out. Girls are 57 per cent and boys are 53 per cent of their final adult height
- gains 1.4–2.3 kg/3–5 lb per year (average weight at four years old is 13.6–17.3 kg/30–38 lb)
- legs grow faster than arms and child looks more grown up
- loses 'baby fat'
- walks up and down stairs using alternate feet
- pedals a trike
- hops on one foot
- catches a bounced ball
- kicks a ball
- can draw a circle, vertical and horizontal lines
- uses tripod grip (two fingers and thumb) on crayons
- builds a tower of seven or more bricks
- sleeps 10 to 12 hours
- eats with little mess
- needs about 1300 calories a day
- carries a cup of drink without spilling
- helps with dressing
- brushes teeth and washes hands
- becomes toilet-trained

- plays realistically with dolls, etc.
- can sort objects into categories of shape or colour
- knows the primary colours by name
- builds a bridge with bricks
- knows 300-1000 words
- understands simple concepts of size and number
- talks in short sentences
- talks to self
- asks repeated questions
- asks for help and tells others what to do
- speech is 80 per cent understandable
- gives own name
- uses more complicated grammar (plurals, adjectives, negatives, prepositions)
- remembers rhymes and songs
- takes turns when playing with other children
- wants to be included in everything
- enjoys make-believe
- develops gender role behaviours

THE FOURTH YEAR TO AGE FIVE

- average weight: 14-18 kg/30-40 lb
- average height: 102-114 cm/40-45 inches
- needs 1700 calories per day
- jumps over small objects
- climbs up almost anything
- sits cross-legged
- threads beads on a string
- copies letters
- writes own name
- repeats telephone number
- counts to 20
- makes up words

- understands simple graduations and sequences
- uses 'in', 'on', 'under'
- understands 'who', 'whose', 'how', 'why'
- understands concept of 'the past'
- knows full name and own sex
- has unpredictable moods
- has imaginary 'friends' and games
- boasts and tells tales
- plays co-operatively but is still selfish
- enjoys being with other children
- manages own toileting – with supervision
- demands to do things unaided

THE FIFTH YEAR TO AGE SIX

- average weight: 17–20.5 kg/37–45 lb
- average height: 107–117 cm/42–46 inches
- pulse rate: 80–110 beats per minute
- respiratory rate: 20–30 breaths per minute
- requires 1700 calories per day
- head size almost equal to an adult's
- normal vision 20/20
- learns to do somersaults
- stands on one foot for 10 seconds
- walks down stairs with alternating feet
- copies squares and triangles
- uses scissors
- walks backwards along a line
- learns to skip
- builds steps with bricks
- understands concepts of size, shape and sequence
- understands quantities (more than, less than)
- uses 1500 words or more
- uses four to seven words to make accurate sentences

- communicates clearly
- knows at least four colours
- makes up jokes
- answers the telephone properly
- uses 'could' and 'would'
- can be generous and caring toward others
- likes asking questions
- learning to blow nose
- prefers one-to-one relationships rather than groups
- follows three-part instructions: 'go upstairs and bring the teddy bear back down again for your sister, please'
- sits still for five minutes
- knows most numbers and letters
- begins to understand time
- uses bricks to make cars, houses, etc.
- can do a 15-piece puzzle

Development over the first five years is all about preparing children to fit in with the rest of society. By the end of this period children should have the following skills in order to be independent enough to cope with school:

- mostly clean and dry
- able to manage own toileting
- responsive to others' needs
- able to concentrate for about 10 minutes
- reasonably obedient
- able to do own buttons and zip up
- co-operative with other children
- able to eat with knife, fork and spoon without mess
- easily understood

It is amazing how many skills are achieved in these first few years and how mature a five year old can be!

2

· · · · ·

Stages and Ages of Development

THE LATER YEARS

Although so much development occurs during the first five years, there are some important areas of maturation and growth still to come, such as:

- learning about moral standards and ideals
- developing a self-image
- understanding abstract concepts and numbers
- developing creative and artistic ability
- becoming aware of the realities of life
- sexual development
- learning to read, write and spell (see Chapter 6)
- developing relationships outside the family (see my book *Families and Friends* in this series).

The years after starting at school and leading into adolescence are exciting. These are the years when children change from having little understanding of what is going on around them to being young people who have a very good idea about the real world. By 12 to 14 years old most children's understanding of right and wrong, of good and bad, of life and death is well developed. This is the stage when children often become idealistic and have a very strong desire to sort out the problems of the world.

   Children develop and change so quickly that it is easy to believe that they are more grown up than they really are. Young children often seem to be very mature and wise and they frequently demand the same freedom as adults. Don't be taken in by this. They have only been around in this world for a short time. When compared with your own experience of life, they have a long way to go!

A reasonable compromise between treating your child as a mature equal and treating him or her more like a baby is to listen carefully to what a young child has to say and then to decide for yourself what you think is best. If you treat children as if they are little adults they will soon take over the home with ever-increasing demands! Small children don't know when to stop and so they have to be told when they have reached the limit.

LEARNING ABOUT RIGHT AND WRONG

Even very young children have some understanding of what is right and wrong. One and a half year olds will reach out to touch something that they know they shouldn't and at the same time look over their shoulder to see how their parents will react. At this stage children become good at saying 'no', but quite often this may actually mean 'yes' and it is clear that there is still considerable confusion and a lack of real understanding.

For the next few years children experiment to find out where the boundary between right and wrong really is. This means that they will deliberately do things that they believe are wrong just to check out if they have got it right. There are some important points for parents to remember about this stage (one to eight years old):

- Children under eight years are still learning about what the standards of right and wrong are.
- It is important to be consistent and clear about where the boundary is between right and wrong.
- Young children may be deliberately disobedient in order to check out were the limit is.
- Children need to be reminded repeatedly about what standard of behaviour is expected of them.

- Disobedient children will respond best to the type of discipline that sets clear standards and encourages learning about what is right, rather than punishment that only tells children that they have done something wrong.

By eight years old most children have gained a pretty good idea about moral standards. Before this time a child will be upset when told off and will be contrite afterwards - often trying to be extra well behaved. However, feelings of guilt only develop gradually. Obvious signs of guilt feelings can be seen in three-year-old children, but it isn't until around eight to nine years that guilt feelings are generated within the child and persist in a rather similar way as they do in adults.

The law recognizes that children only gradually understand right and wrong. Children less than eight years old cannot be held responsible for their actions in any way. Children 10 to 14 years old can be held to have some responsibility for their actions, but are not considered criminally responsible. It is only after 14 years of age that the law judges a child to be able to have a clear understanding of right and wrong and therefore to be criminally responsible. Even then, children with criminal convictions are dealt with quite separately from the prison and probation system that deals with adults.

It is all too easy to forget that children go on learning about right and wrong for many years (this is true of adults, too!). Don't give up too quickly, because children need continuous teaching about right and wrong if they are going to fit in with the rest of society and have reasonable standards of behaviour.

Children also need to be taught how to be kind, generous and thoughtful about the needs of others. This is called altruism and it gradually develops over several years. Three- to four-year-old children usually show some signs of being able to recognize the needs of others, but rarely respond to them. Eight to 10 year olds may have an understanding of other people's feelings, but they are still much more concerned about themselves most of the time.

However, by 14 years old most children have gained a very clear idea about the feelings of others and will generally respond positively to them.

DEVELOPING A SELF-IMAGE AND SELF-ESTEEM

Babies are able to distinguish between themselves and the outside world quite soon after birth, but it isn't until around six months old that babies begin to make a clear distinction between themselves and other people. The process of becoming a separate individual continues gradually, step by step. By 18 months most children are beginning to have a mind of their own and say 'no' with some conviction.

Not long after two years old, children begin to say 'I' rather than calling themselves by their Christian name as if they were talking about somebody else. By two and a half years old most children reach another important stage in the way they see themselves as separate beings. This can be shown by their ability to recognize themselves in photographs or by the 'mirror test':

1. Put a mark on a toddler's forehead.
2. Stand the child in front of a mirror.
3. Children younger than two years will rub the mirror to remove the mark.
4. Children over the age of three years will rub the mark off their own face.

This means that if you tell a two year old that he is a failure, he won't take much notice. But if you were to tell a four-year-old child that he has done badly he usually becomes upset, although he soon bounces back and doesn't take it to heart. Tell a seven year old that he is a failure and a bad boy and it won't take long before that child comes to see himself as bad – a real failure.

It isn't until six to eight years old that children begin to understand what they are like as people – what type of people they are:

- clever or not too clever
- good-looking or unattractive
- successful or a failure
- likable or disliked
- generous or mean
- and so on.

This is a gradual process that takes several years. For some children it may happen rather earlier than usual, either because a child is advanced in development or because the child has been repeatedly told what kind of person he or she is. Hence the danger of saying negative things to children because they will come to believe that they are true.

Self-esteem is to do with that part of self-image that describes how good or bad a person feels. It is strongly linked with how 'good' children feel they are. By eight years of age most children will have developed a self-image, which is to a large extent dependent on how other people react to them. Positive reactions to children will help to build up high self-esteem, negative reactions quite the opposite.

An interesting natural experiment on the development of self-image occurred about 40 years ago when it was first possible to determine the sex of a child by checking the chromosomes at birth. Before that time a few babies were given the incorrect sex at birth because the genitalia were abnormal.

Chromosome tests revealed that some children had been brought up as the wrong sex. In these cases an operation was carried out to correct the abnormality and to change the sex of the child so that it fitted with the chromosomes. It was found that it was possible to change the sex of a child up to the age of seven to eight years, without any problem. However, after eight to nine years old, children continued to feel that they were the same sex that they had been brought up as - even if everything was done to change their anatomy, their name and their style of dress.

Fortunately this would not happen today, because if there is any doubt it is always possible to check the chromosomes while the baby is still very young. These findings confirm that children develop a fairly clear self-image of themselves around six to eight years and that once this has formed, it can be very difficult to change.

Adolescence is another important period for the development of self-image. Although children normally have a good idea of what kind of people they are by the time they are eight years old, there is a period of review during adolescence. This is a stage when teenagers often spend a lot of time looking at themselves in the mirror and trying out a whole range of clothes and different ways of behaving.

Self-image is formed mainly by the way that people respond to you. For example, if people generally react to a child in a negative and hostile way, it is unlikely to lead to a good self-image. On the other hand, if you continually praise a child whatever the circumstances, the child will develop a very good self-image.

It is actually possible to give too much praise and encouragement to children with the result that they become over-confident and unaware of their weaknesses. On the whole, however, we don't give enough encouragement and positive attention to children when they do well and as a result most children have a lower self-esteem than they should have.

Remember how parents get excited and tell anyone who will listen every little thing that their baby has done? Yet after a year or two it is difficult to keep up the same level of praise and enthusiasm and much easier to be critical of any mistakes.

There is now good evidence that children with generally high self-esteem do better and are good at surviving and being happy if they are under stress, compared with children who have low self-esteem. At the same time there is evidence that children who feel bad about themselves will tend to behave badly. Delinquency, non-attendance

29

at school and drug abuse are closely related to poor self-image and low self-esteem.

UNDERSTANDING ABSTRACT CONCEPTS

Before eight to 10 years of age most children think in a rather factual and reality-based way. For example, they will think of a table as something solid to put things on. Abstract ideas are much more complicated and develop slowly. An abstract concept involving a table might be about flatness, or about how a surface requires support in at least three different points if it is to stand alone, or how the force of gravity is counteracted by an equal force exerted by the table top.

Young children have little understanding of abstract concepts. For example, the concept of danger takes a while to develop. At first it is a reaction to things that can be seen such as fire and water. However, if the danger can't be seen (as in deep water or unlit matches), youngsters won't be able to understand the risks involved.

By the age of four to six years children begin to understand that there is more to the world around them than meets the eye, but they are easily confused about what is real and what is imaginary. Objects like tables and chairs may be thought to have a life of their own. So it isn't surprising that at this age children are easily scared of imaginary monsters and mysterious happenings.

Mathematics is a good example of the overlap between abstract and concrete ideas. As soon as children aged six to eight years move away from counting beads or fingers to try multiplication and division, it becomes more difficult to think of numbers in a concrete way. Problem-solving requires a special grasp of basic number concepts together with the ability to reason in a logical way. The use of abstract concepts is often helpful in this process. Ten to 12 year olds are beginning to use abstract ideas in this way.

Later on - and carrying on into adolescence - children begin to understand even more abstract ideas such as beauty, forgiveness or generosity. There are many similar concepts and none of them is easy even for adults to understand fully. They certainly keep philosophers busy. So don't be surprised if your child also finds these abstract ideas difficult to grasp.

DEVELOPING CREATIVE AND ARTISTIC ABILITY

There are interesting stages of development that show how children see the world. The first sign of creativity can be found in the way children use their imagination at play. Play bricks become houses or cars, dolls become real people and empty boxes can take on a life of their own.

There is a wide range of individual variation in how creative children are. This depends on a number of factors:

- Children become more creative with age.
- Time, equipment and space are needed.
- Children respond to encouragement to be creative.
- Setting an example of creativity helps.
- Creativity may run in families.
- Watching the TV probably reduces creative activity.
- Having high self-esteem increases creative output.
- Some children have a naturally creative temperament.

Some toys can encourage creativity and stimulate the imagination. These are toys that leave a lot to the imagination and that can be used in various ways. Empty cartons, plastic bottles and wooden bricks are more likely to develop creativity in children than manufactured toys that are complete in every detail.

Children's art is a good way of following how their imagination is developing. Two-year-old children enjoy scribbling that has little shape or form to it. Soon this takes the form of lines and circles and by three and a half years old these shapes begin to have a special meaning for the child. By four years old most children are able to

31

draw a simple face with a few recognizable features such as eyes and a mouth.

By five years old the face usually has arms and legs coming out of it but often lacks a body. The body soon arrives but the arms are in the wrong place at first and the head is large in relation to the rest of the body. Later on, the picture of a person becomes more accurate, with more features. By eight years old the body usually has a neck and shoulders with arms attached to them. Most of us don't progress much further than this stage, where the drawing fits closely with reality. It is necessary to work very hard in order to improve drawing skills beyond those of a 10 year old.

At around five to six years old children begin to draw houses and other familiar outdoor scenes. At first the sky is very high and there is a gap between it and the ground. Gradually the sky moves towards the ground; the sky and ground meet up at around eight to nine years of age. This is the stage when children are able to draw realistically. However, it isn't until children are entering adolescence that they are able to make accurate perspective drawings.

BECOMING AWARE OF THE REALITIES OF LIFE

Although it is impossible to remember exactly what it was like to b e a tiny baby and most of us can't remember much before three years old, our memories probably reflect what it was like at the time. It seems likely that young children live in a world that is rather like a dream, where time doesn't obey any of the usual rules and where the boundary between real and unreal is not at all distinct.

Up to the age of three to four years children have a special type of memory called 'idetic' or 'photographic' memory. Things are remembered more as pictures than words – rather like a dream. Young children often show an astonishing ability to remember places they have been to only once many months previously and may be able to give detailed directions when travelling by car.

This special photographic memory ability is gradually lost in

2-3

3-4

4-5

5-6

6-7

7+

10+

most children as they begin to talk more. Memories become gradually more verbal than visual, although some children continue to have a memory that is better for pictures and images than for words.

The change from visual to verbal memory mirrors the gradual development of an understanding of the real world as we know it. It is interesting that in older children visual information is stored mainly in the side of the brain that is non-dominant or less active, while verbal memory is stored mainly in the dominant side of the brain – that is, the side that controls speech and the dominant hand.

The division of visual and more imaginative activity on one side of the brain and more basic, down-to-earth, verbal activity on the other seems to help the brain to be more efficient. It helps to avoid the problem of similar messages from both sides of the brain becoming confused.

Children under seven to nine years old find it difficult to understand reality as we know it. Their concept of time, of position or place, of people and individuals is still developing. Young children easily become confused about what is true and what is false, and what is good and bad.

Because most young children have only a limited grasp of reality, it may seem as though they often tell 'lies'. However, fact and fantasy are easily mixed up together and it is only gradually that they learn about the real world and about truth.

Some of the truths about the real world that children discover are unpleasant and may well be distressing. For example, children of seven to nine years old develop a much clearer idea of their own weaknesses and begin to see the failings of themselves and their parents and teachers. Exposure to news of disasters headlined in the press, on radio and TV probably has a greater impact on children at this stage of development than might be expected.

Young children easily pick up their parents' emotions and their reactions are a reflection of their parents' behaviour. Older children have a much better understanding of the reality of events and they develop their own personal reactions rather than just being a mirror of their parents' responses.

Children have to learn about the 'wicked ways of the world', but the timing and amount of the exposure are important. Children less than about seven years old will have only a limited intellectual understanding of what is going on. However, they will be acutely aware of how the adults around them are reacting and will pick up all their emotions.

If children are exposed to distressing events early on in life they can easily become confused about what is really going on. The more distressed their parents are, the more upset they will be themselves. It is therefore helpful to give simple explanations to young children about what is really happening, without going into too much detail - which only causes more confusion.

SEXUAL DEVELOPMENT

It might be thought that sexual development doesn't start until puberty. In fact it starts from the moment of conception and from then on there are a number of important stages, each of which is a delicate balance between male and female influences. These are the main stages:

1. Chromosomal Sex

The sex chromosomes (XX for female and XY for male) determine the reproductive glands or gonads that begin to form soon after conception. About 1 in 500 children have some abnormality of the sex chromosomes which results in developmental and learning problems.

2. Gonadal Sex

The ovary in girls or the testes in boys are determined by the sex chromosomes. They produce the sex hormones in small amounts until puberty, when production shoots up to high levels.

3. Hormonal Sex

The hormones determine the external genitalia (the penis or the vagina and clitoris). Occasionally the genitals may develop abnormally before birth, for instance if the mother has been given hormones or if for some reason the baby is producing abnormal hormone levels.

4. Genital Sex

The sex of a baby is determined by the appearance of the external genitals and can be seen by a scan test before birth. Very rarely their development is abnormal and then the baby's sex has to be checked by looking at the chromosomes.

5. Gender Identity

By three years old most children will be able to tell you whether they are a boy or a girl. This is determined by what their parents and other people say. So it would be possible for a girl to be brought up as a boy and then by three years old to believe that she was a boy, but at this stage the identity could still be changed. By five to seven years old gender identity is gradually becoming more fixed and, by eight years old, cannot be changed.

6. Gender Role

Expectations from society and the family play an important part in determining how children take up a male or female role. However, animal studies show that hormones both before and after birth also have an effect on male/female behaviour.

7. Sexual Identity

The development of heterosexual or homosexual identity is a process that takes place towards the end of adolescence and is largely determined by all the earlier stages of sexual development.

8. Sexual Role

Finally, the way people behave within a sexual relationship is determined by a wide range of factors including previous experience, self-image, physical and emotional state and the characteristics of their partner.

Sexual development starts in a very physical way that is fixed and difficult to change. Then, as you can see from the outline above, it becomes gradually more psychological, responsive to the outside world and open to change. The main thing to understand about sexual development is that it is a gradual process that starts at conception and continues into adulthood. It is not something that is over and done with in just a few years during adolescence.

CONCLUSION

Although most of the obvious stages of development have been reached by the time children start at school, the less obvious development of an understanding of the self and the outside world continues over the next few years. By adolescence all the most important stages of development have normally been achieved. Therefore adolescence is mainly a time of consolidation of earlier development. But development continues well into adult life with each person's ever-increasing understanding of the relationships and interactions between the outside world and the inner world and between people and ideas.

3

. . . . .

Understanding Development

Growth, development and maturation are not the same thing. Growth means that there is an increase in quantity - such as in height or weight. Development suggests that there is a change in the complexity of the child. A change in quality rather than quantity. For example, a new skill or ability develops.

Maturation, on the other hand, applies to a biological change that is not affected by outside influences and is therefore difficult to stop or even to delay. Puberty is a good example of a maturational change that occurs even if a child's development is delayed in other ways.

There are several general points about development that need to be kept in mind as you read through this book:

- The rate of growth, development and maturation is at its fastest during the first few weeks and months of life. Then there is another spurt of rapid change during adolescence.
- Development is a continuous process, but often occurs at a variable rate, making progress by going two steps forward followed by a pause or even a step backwards before moving ahead again.
- Each individual skill or ability develops at a different time and rate from the others.
- There is a definite sequence of development. For example, walking occurs before running. Understanding occurs before talking.
- Once a developmental stage has been reached it can be lost again under the influences of physical or emotional stress.

- Each individual child has his or her own unique developmental progression, both in the rate at which change occurs and in its pattern.
- It is possible to make some predictions from early development about what progress a child will make later on.
- Development is an interactive process. It depends on the influence of the environment, the child's genetic make-up and the child's ability to learn from experience.

Don't worry if it all seems a bit complicated at this stage. This isn't surprising because nobody understands everything about the way children grow and change. In any case it is possible to help your child's development go smoothly without having to know all the details about it. I will outline the main points that are likely to be of use to you.

'NORMAL' DEVELOPMENT

Although we all talk about what is normal and what is abnormal, it isn't as straightforward as it might seem. In fact, some people find the word 'normal' so unsatisfactory that they prefer not to use it at all. The various meanings of 'normal' include:

- the most frequently occurring
- statistically average
- usual and expected
- typical and standard
- occurring within certain limits
- conforming to a convention.

When I mention 'normal' development in this book I will be referring to what happens to most children. There will always be some children who don't fit into this pattern and who are very different from 'normal'. Abnormal or atypical development is

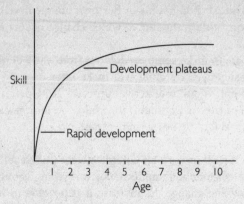

Figure 1: A typical developmental curve

outside this 'normal' range, but this doesn't necessarily mean that it is 'pathological' or a sign that something is wrong. For example, Mozart was a brilliant musician at the age of seven years, which was quite outside the normal range and therefore very abnormal. But this doesn't mean that he had a problem or suffered from a disorder of development!

One of the chief characteristics of development is that it is progressive – moving steadily from one stage to the next. Each stage is more complicated than the last. The rate of development is fastest early on and then it gradually tails off to a steady level or plateau, as shown in Figure 1.

When children are still very young and the rate of development is rapid it is easy to see how a slight change in age can produce a great change in skill (Figure 2).

This explains why such large differences can occur between one child's development and another early on in life, and yet they both fall within the normal range. This also explains why some children appear to be little geniuses because their skills seem to be so advanced, although they may be only a bit ahead in terms of developmental age (Figure 3).

It is therefore extremely difficult to predict accurately whether

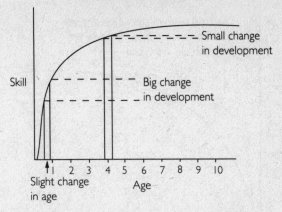

Figure 2: The change in development at different ages

or not a child is 'normal' in those first few months. Unless, of course, it is very obviously different. However, by seven to eight years old, when most skills have been established, it is usually possible to make quite accurate predictions from the way that children are developing and then to determine what level of ability they are likely to have later on in life.

There are several different ways in which development can make progress (see also Figures 4a, b and c):

1. *Normal Development.* General development is within the normal range. The children can be expected to cope on their own as adults and live independent lives.
2. *Mild Developmental Delay.* All development is slower than normal. The child will have general learning difficulties and will require some support and guidance as an adult. This is outside the normal range of development.
3. *Moderate or Severe Developmental Delay.* General development is so slow that the affected children will need almost continuous supervision throughout the rest of their lives.
4. *Specific Developmental Delay.* The development of one or more skills is slow enough to require special help, but the rest of the

41

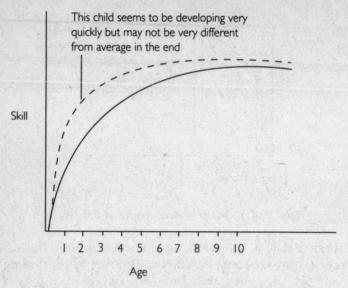

This child seems to be developing very quickly but may not be very different from average in the end

Skill

1 2 3 4 5 6 7 8 9 10

Age

Figure 3: Big changes occur when children are young

child's general development is within the normal range.
5. *Developmental Regression.* It is rare for development to go backwards or regress, but severe physical stress - such as an infection - or emotional upset - such as bereavement - can do this in the short term.

These different paths that development can follow are usually set early on in a child's life and there is a limit to how much the course of a child's development can be changed. On the other hand, it is quite easy to make really big advances in development in a short space of time if a child is given the right sort of help. But in the long run this may not make that much difference.

The complicated process of development is easier to understand if you can imagine a threshold: below this threshold a child lacks a particular skill, but once the threshold is crossed the child has achieved the skill (Figure 5).

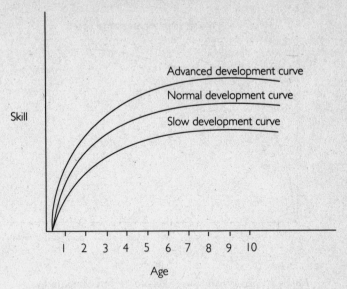

Figure 4a: Every child's development occurs at a different rate

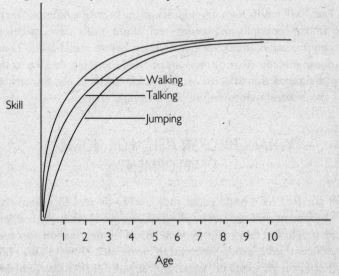

Figure 4b: Not all skills develop at the same rate

43

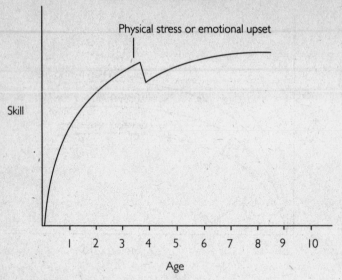

Figure 4c: Stress can cause skills to be lost temporarily

Each skill has its own developmental curve with a different shape to it. For example, movement and motor skills develop before communication ability, speech develops before social skills. There is some evidence that the various parts of the brain develop at the same time as the different skills. So, for example, the motor area of the brain develops before the language area.

WHAT CHILDREN NEED FOR NORMAL DEVELOPMENT

All children have basic needs that have to be met to ensure that development will progress well. Children are remarkably resilient and tough. It takes quite extreme stress or deprivation to cause significant, long-lasting problems in most cases. However, if a child is not given an adequate amount of any of the seven basic needs,

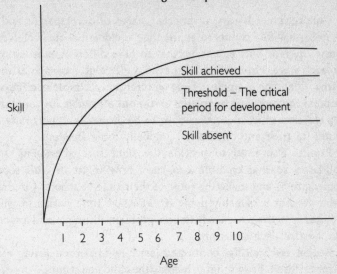

Figure 5: Development goes through a critical period when a skill is achieved

the result will probably be a delay in development.

A CHILD'S SEVEN BASIC NEEDS
1. Protection from physical, emotional and moral danger
2. Nourishment and protection from the elements
3. Consistent, loving care and affection
4. Age-appropriate social training
5. Attention to needs at different stages of development
6. Assistance toward eventual independence
7. Fair and clear limit-setting for behaviour

Some of these basic needs are very obvious and it isn't difficult to see how a child who is malnourished or physically ill-treated will fail to thrive. The child's need for clear and consistent discipline is not quite so apparent, although a disobedient child may eventually slip behind with progress at school and find developing relationships especially difficult.

Children's needs vary at different stages of development and it is necessary for parents to adjust their childcare as their children grow up. Not only is it important to have different expectations at each stage, but children also need a different approach as they grow older. For example, young children need almost continuous supervision and can't be trusted to stay out of trouble for very long. As children grow older they have to be given the opportunity to build up trust and be allowed gradually more freedom.

Parents also need to provide the right sort of training and guidance so that children can learn how to fit in with social expectations and make the most of their time at school. Children who are not reasonably polite or who take little notice of what adults say to them are likely to have problems fitting in and making the best of each situation.

Recent research has confirmed just how important loving care is for children. In addition to helping the child feel secure, a positive and affectionate relationship leads to the development of a good self-esteem, which is one of the main factors that helps children to develop well even if all the odds are against them.

WHAT INFLUENCES CHILDREN'S DEVELOPMENT?

The stages of growth and development that children pass through are to a large extent predetermined and the majority of development has already occurred by the time a child is born. All the basic structures are in place at birth and modern research keeps finding that there is more that babies can do than was ever thought possible.

However, even before birth there are a number of factors that can influence the way in which the baby grows and matures. These factors are at work right the way though the child's life and on into adulthood. Here are some of the most important ones:

- individual constitutional make-up
- genetic influences
- physical stress
- emotional upset
- deprivation of basic needs
- lack of adequate stimulation
- training and teaching
- social and cultural expectations.

Many of these factors can have a negative influence and disrupt development. But some of them can also have a positive effect and result in a strengthening influence for a child. For example, the emotional stress of bereavement could make a child feel very distressed at the time, but if children manage to cope well with the experience they are likely to be stronger emotionally and better able to deal with any future loss. In the same way a child who has had measles will have a stronger resistance to infection by the measles virus in future.

Each child's individual characteristics are already well established before birth and are largely under the influence of the child's unique genetic make-up. Other factors can also affect children's development before birth, including infections, lack of oxygen, the mother's state of health, and a range of chemical substances. The characteristics that a child is born with are naturally due to a mixture of genetic and environmental factors. Together they make up the child's constitution.

Physical stress due to infection, injury or other factors can delay development by affecting the child as a whole and causing general ill-health. On the other hand, the physical stress may be very specific and affect the development of just one part of the body. An infection of the urine could, for example, delay the development of bladder control. Injury to the nerves of the muscles in the legs might lead to delay in a child's learning to walk.

Emotional distress may be less obvious than the physical problems that delay development, but the effects can be just as severe.

Usually emotional upset is generalized, affecting several different aspects of the child's behaviour. The distress must be severe or prolonged if it is to affect development. For example, if a child is seriously depressed and miserable for more than a week or two, all aspects of development are likely to slow down, along with an associated disturbance of sleep, appetite and concentration.

Although development will continue even if nothing is done to help it on its way, it certainly helps to provide the right sort of environment for children to grow up in. However, too much stimulation and excessive training can actually interfere with development. For example, very bright children are sometimes given a great deal of academic teaching from an early age, which may have the effect of speeding up some parts of their development but may cause other parts, such as learning about practical skills and relationships, not to develop properly.

Social and cultural influences also affect children's development. Afro-Caribbean children tend to develop their skills of movement and co-ordination at an earlier age than do white children. Burmese children are trained not to show their feelings and so the development of emotional expression is comparatively slow. Many of the differences between boys and girls have been thought to be due to social expectations, but there is now more evidence that constitutional variations have a major influence on differences in development. For example, boys tend to develop more aggressive behaviour than girls due to differences in their hormonal make-up as well as (often) the expectations of their parents. Nevertheless there is very good evidence that right from an early age boys and girls are treated differently.

INDIVIDUAL DIFFERENCES IN DEVELOPMENT

There is amazing variation between children. Even identical twins may be remarkably unlike each other. The behaviour of new-born babies is highly individual. Here are some of the ways in which infants have been found to differ from each other:

- activity level
- irritability
- sucking and mouthing habits
- alertness
- eating and sleeping patterns
- regularity and predictability
- adaptability to change
- amount and intensity of crying.

Each child has a unique combination of these and other temperamental characteristics. The last three on the list above have been shown to be linked to difficult personalities and problem behaviour in young children. So if you have a child who demonstrated the following behaviours at birth and has continued with them ever since, you will probably have had a hard time!

1. Unpredictability and irregularity
2. Slowness to adapt to change
3. Intense, mainly negative emotions.

Children who have these temperamental characteristics present from birth are likely to be more difficult to look after and to have a stormy developmental progress over the first few years. Fortunately many children grow out of these problem behaviours as they grow older. Parents can make a positive outcome more likely by being 'super parents'. For example, these 'difficult' children need a great deal of warm affection and at the same time they also need very clear and consistent discipline and training.

Differences in temperament are at first largely due to genetic factors, but as children grow older the effect of the outside world becomes more and more powerful. It is possible for the child's experience of life to make major changes to how that child thinks, feels and behaves.

The differences between development in boys and girls are notice-able, to say the least. But in the end it is the differences between individual children that is more striking than whether they are male or female. Or, to put it another way, there are more differences between children as individuals than between boys and girls as a whole.

Parents are only too aware of how children can influence the way in which they themselves react. A placid, easy-going child will probably provoke very different feelings and behaviour from adults than one who is constantly demanding and whose emotions and reactions are unpredictable. Interactions between parents and their children play a major part in how children develop. It is these interactions between children and the world around them that in the end has the strongest effect on development.

Older children have been shown to vary in a number of characteristics that tend to persist over time and not change very much as development progresses. Here are some of the more important features that have a strong tendency to persist and not change much with time:

- ability to solve problems
- shyness and sociability
- aggressiveness
- sleep and eating habits
- curiosity
- demonstration of affection
- clumsiness.

With these obvious individual differences between children it is easy to see how they could become labelled 'shy', 'aggressive', 'distant', etc., labels which might then become stuck with the child and further limit the scope for change. For example, a clumsy boy could easily have the whole family expecting him to drop something at any moment. He may then do just this and confirm that he is indeed uncoordinated. Everyone is then happy: the family know that they were right to call the boy clumsy and the boy himself feels that at least he is playing his role as 'the clumsy one' and keeping everyone happy.

The differences in the rate of development between one child and another have already been referred to and will be discussed in more detail in Chapter 7. In most cases each child will continue at his or her own individual developmental rate and, although it is possible to make changes in the short term, it is much more difficult to make long-term changes. For example, it is quite easy to train a child to walk earlier than normal, but in the long run it is unlikely that the child will walk any better than anyone else or become an Olympic walker as a result!

CONCLUSION

Each child has a unique developmental pattern that depends on a wide range of different factors. Parents can do a lot to help their children to make good progress and to make the most of their abilities. But there is a limit to what can be done to change the course of a child's developmental progress, which is to a large extent determined very early on in life.

4
. . . . .

Emotional Development

BABIES' FEELINGS

It is very difficult to tell exactly what a new-born baby is feeling, and even as children grow older they still find it hard to put their feelings into words. Which isn't surprising because adults aren't that good at it either! However, the difficulty of knowing what young children are feeling has led parents to try and guess. It is easy to think that when a baby cries it could be due to serious emotional distress. While this could be true, it is more often *not* the case. Crying is one of the main ways that babies have of communicating and the clever baby doesn't take long to discover that crying quickly brings him or her full adult attention.

The crying of a new-born baby can actually be very reassuring for parents because the yelling lets everyone know that the baby is alive and strong. However, most babies spend much of their waking time crying and it is easy to feel worried that the baby is upset. The strong feelings that parents experience when they hear their baby cry are helpful because crying is a signal that the baby wants attention. However, the crying often develops in an unhelpful way when children use crying to manipulate their parents.

The skill of emotional manipulation develops early on in life. In fact, manipulating people by using emotional pressure is a very primitive way of getting what you want. It is amazing how quickly even very young children learn the art of manipulation. It is important to recognize it for what it is and to help children to develop more acceptable ways of making their needs known. Older children and adults who continue to be manipulative and use emotional pressure in a big way are difficult to live with and seldom learn how to relate to others in acceptable, productive ways.

WHICH EMOTION IS WHICH?

Although it has been claimed that babies have a range of different types of crying, each with a particular meaning, most parents find it quite difficult to tell one from the other. On the other hand it is easy to tell the difference between a baby who is mildly distressed and one who has become really worked up, even though it may only be because his or her meal hasn't arrived exactly on time!

Very young babies can only show their emotions by quietly gurgling and smiling or by crying and screaming. It seems likely that a baby's emotions are indeed quite simple and not at all clearly defined. When a baby cries it is difficult to tell if he or she is anxious, sad, angry, has indigestion or is just bored and wants some attention. It isn't until four to six weeks old that the evidence of a definite and clear-cut emotion is seen, when a baby starts to smile.

All people generally experience two types of emotions: positive (enjoyable) and negative (unpleasant) emotions, as you can see from the list below:

Positive	**Negative**
calmness and relaxation	fear and anxiety
love and affection	hate and anger
happiness and excitement	sadness and depression

Each positive emotion has its mirror image – a negative aspect of the same emotion. So for example, it is possible to cry with happiness. Love can easily turn to hate and it isn't unusual to experience remarkably strong feelings of anger towards those whom we also love the most. Another example of the mixing together of opposite emotions can be seen in the way some people react to anxiety by appearing to be very relaxed, even to the point of almost being unable to move.

There are, of course, other more complicated emotions such as jealousy and humour, but they are not 'pure' emotions and are made up of several different feelings. Jealousy, for example, includes both anxiety and anger. Because these 'mixed' emotions are so complicated I will concentrate mainly on those that I have listed above.

New-born babies obviously have both positive and negative feelings, but it is difficult to tell exactly which type of emotion is being experienced at any time. When babies smile, can you tell if it is due to feeling happy or to feeling affectionate – or could it just be wind? When a baby cries, can you tell if it is due to pain, anger or anxiety? Most people find it very difficult to be sure about exactly what a baby is feeling at any time. But as children grow up, their emotions gradually develop.

The first 'smile' may be seen soon after birth, but these smiles are not the real thing since they often occur when the child is completely relaxed or even asleep. By two weeks old it may be possible to elicit a smile by any form of gentle stimulation, although the smile often occurs as much as eight seconds after the event. By about six weeks babies are smiling in direct response to sounds (especially their mother's voice) and to smiling faces. Even eyes on their own can produce smiling and the reaction time gradually becomes less as time goes by. By eight weeks the child's smiling becomes part of developing a social relationship.

Laughter is usually heard for the first time at around four months of age, as a reaction to strong stimulation by touch, sound or movement. By nine months laughter becomes more responsive to social situations such as hiding games or behaving in a very different way from usual. However, at this stage the same behaviour may result in either laughter or in tears.

Older children gradually develop a sense of humour and by six to nine years most children have found their own unique brand of humour. At this stage children go through a phase of loving jokes that almost no one else finds funny!

THE DEVELOPMENT OF FEAR AND ANXIETY

Even very young babies show some signs of fear, but it is in a very uncomplicated form and is seen when children react with a startle to a loud noise or any sudden or unexpected change in the world around them. But it isn't until about six to eight months old that children show the first absolutely clear evidence that they are experiencing a definite emotion. At about six months old the first signs of anxiety appear in the form of anxiety towards strangers and fear of separation (see my book *Worries and Fears* in this series).

When a child clings to his or her mother and refuses to be passed over to a stranger to be held, you can be sure that the child is experiencing anxiety. The fact that this doesn't usually happen until a child is at least six months old isn't an indication that younger children don't experience any anxiety at all. But it does mean that children younger than six months probably have unformed and undeveloped feelings of anxiety that can't be expressed in a very clear way.

Anxiety is therefore the first negative emotion to develop in a specific way so that it is absolutely clear what the child is feeling. Anxiety is experienced in a very physical way and is associated with a high level of physiological arousal. It is this heightened arousal that causes the following symptoms:

- palpitations and racing heartbeat
- sweating
- tense muscles and muscle pains
- shaking and loss of co-ordination
- dry mouth and blurred eye sight
- 'fuzzy' head and fainting
- poor concentration
- stomach upset and breathing problems
- frequent visits to the toilet
- disturbed sleep and appetite.

It would be unusual - and certainly very uncomfortable - for one person to experience all these symptoms. In fact, each individual has his or her own particular way of reacting physically to worries and fears. Young children complain a lot about the physical symptoms of anxiety. Then as they grow older, their complaints become more specific and easier to relate to their worries. The list below gives an idea about how children's symptoms of anxiety change with age:

two to six years: general aches and pains
five to 10: leg aches
six to 12: tummy aches
seven to 14: headaches

As well as the change with age, symptoms also vary a great deal from one individual to another. However, all children are likely to experience unsettled sleep and to have a disturbed appetite if they experience significant worries or anxiety - whatever their age might be.

Children's fears tend to change as they grow older. At first the worries are to do with real dangers and specific objects, but later on in adolescence the anxiety becomes more to do with the imagination and ideas, as you can see from the list below:

- birth onwards: loud noises
- six months to three years: strangers
- nine months onwards: high places
- two to four years: animals
- four to six years: darkness, storms, imaginary monsters
- six to 12 years: mysterious happenings, ghosts
- 12 to 18 years: social embarrassment, academic failure, death and wars

THE DEVELOPMENT OF ANGER

The first sign of obvious anger directed against a specific person develops between 18 months and two years of age. Before that time children will scream and yell in what seems an angry way, but it is not usually personal. It is more likely to be aimed at the situation than the person. For example, if a toy is taken away from a one-year-old child, there will probably be a lot of angry screaming directed at nobody in particular. But take the same toy from a three year old and the anger will clearly be aimed at the person who took it away.

In order to be 'properly' angry it is necessary to be aware of oneself as separate from other people and from the rest of the outside world. This stage is not reached until between two and three years of age. This coincides with the time when children start to use 'I' when talking about themselves, rather than their name:

18 months: 'Want it'
24 months: 'Francis want it'
30 months: 'I want it'

At first, anger is shown in a physical way by pushing, hitting, kicking and rolling on the floor, but by the time children are four to six years old, their anger is expressed more often in words. At the same time their outbursts of anger become shorter. At least the violent part doesn't last as long as it used to and is replaced with sulking instead. So children continue to react to frustration with anger in one form or another and the outbursts probably last much the same time. However, the way in which the anger is expressed changes as children grow older.

Whenever a child is angry there will always be a great deal of anxiety mixed in with it - and the same applies to adults as well. Do you remember the last time that you were really angry? Didn't you feel panicky and shaky at the same time? This means that anger is always associated with the same symptoms that occur in anxiety (listed on page 55).

THE DEVELOPMENT OF SADNESS AND DEPRESSION

Although children can become sad and miserable in a reasonably clear way from around two years old, this is not the same as being depressed. Young children easily show signs of sadness, but it doesn't last for long and they soon bounce back again as if nothing much has happened. At first children pick up sadness by copying what their parents say and do. In the same way that a three year old will join in adult laughter about something that he or she doesn't understand, so too can a child copy sadness without really knowing quite what it is about.

Depression is different from sadness because it has two additional essential components that are not necessarily part of feeling miserable:

Depression = Feelings of worthlessness (concept of self)
          = Feelings of hopelessness (concept of time)

Children who feel depressed come to believe that they are useless failures and that there is little hope that things will get better in the future. In order to feel a failure and to have a sense of worthlessness, it is necessary to have a concept of what sort of person you are (self-concept) and this doesn't develop until around seven to eight years old. A sense of hopelessness requires a concept of time and this doesn't develop until around the same age of seven to eight years.

All this may sound rather theoretical, but it should fit in with your own observations of children. For example, most children are not able to tell the time properly until they are at least seven years old and it is very unusual for a child younger than seven to feel a failure for more than a few minutes.

This means that it would be very rare for a child of less than eight years old to become 'depressed' in the strict sense of the word. Younger children can certainly be sad and tearful, but that isn't the same as the emotion of depression, which has a very different significance.

Any child who is depressed will also have angry and anxious feelings mixed in with it. All the symptoms of anxiety (listed on page 55) will also be present. In addition to the anxiety symptoms, depressed children also have symptoms of anger such as irritability and being self-centered. It is easy to miss depression in children because the signs of anger or anxiety may be more obvious than the underlying depression.

I have used the word 'depression' to describe a very specific mood state that is part of the normal range of emotions of older children and adults. This is quite different from a depressive disorder or illness where the depression is so strong that it actually takes over control of the person. However, the symptoms and signs of a depressive disorder are much the same as those described above. The main difference is that a depressive disorder is so severe that it is a significant handicap and interferes with everyday life.

THE DEVELOPMENT OF GRIEF

Grief is the normal emotional reaction to loss. The most obvious form of grief is seen in the bereavement reaction to the death of a close friend or relative, but the same reaction also occurs after the loss of a pet or if a friend moves away to another area. Surprisingly strong grief reactions may also be felt when an older brother or sister leaves home.

Very young children show little or no sign of grief provided that their everyday life is not unsettled and they are being well looked after. Before seven to eight years old, children have little understanding of death and what it means. However, they quickly pick up how other people are feeling and react to that.

However, children over the age of about six months do show definite short-term reactions to separation from a parent and the level of distress that is caused increases to a peak at around three to four years. There are three phases for the response to separation:

1. protest: crying, screaming and actively searching for the absent parent
2. withdrawal: becoming detached and quiet, showing few emotions
3. despair: resignation, misery and listlessness.

As children grow older these three phases of emotional reaction to separation develop into the bereavement reaction, which also has three stages:

1. shock and disbelief (lasts up to two weeks)
2. overwhelming emotions (lasts up to six weeks)
3. readjustment (lasts up to one year).

Bereavement reactions in older children have more to do with ideas and thinking processes than the early separation responses of very young children. Bereaved children under the age of eight years may well show signs of grief but they can quickly put it aside and appear quite happy. It is important to realize that this isn't because young children are hard-hearted and unfeeling, it is because they are too young to understand what death means and that it is different from someone going away on holiday.

In order to understand death children need to have reached the stage of development where they have a concept of time and a concept of self. The concept of time is needed to understand that death is for ever. A concept of self is necessary for children to realize that each individual is unique and can't be replaced. Both these concepts are reasonably well developed by the age of seven to eight, but not before, unless the child's development is very advanced.

Some children may appear to understand about death at a very young age, but they are probably just copying what they have heard and seen, rather than having a proper understanding. Children who are delayed in their development will naturally take that much longer to come to terms with what death and loss are all about.

Grief is not the same thing as depression because self-esteem is normally preserved and there are no feelings of worthlessness, but in other respects the symptoms and signs are much the same. Grief contains large amounts of anger, guilt and anxiety, which may seem an odd way to react to bereavement but exactly the same emotions are mixed together in depression.

So bereaved children show grief in different ways at different stages of their development. Before seven to eight years of age children may show very little response to a personal loss, provided that their basic needs for care and affection are being met. Young children tend to take their cue from adults and to a large extent they mirror the emotions and behaviour of those around them. Older children can experience the full range of grief and in adolescence the experience of loss can result in the most acute feelings of any age.

DELAYED EMOTIONAL DEVELOPMENT

Some children seem to take much longer to develop mature emotions. If the delay is marked then such children are not difficult to recognize because they have the following problems:

- easily upset
- often irritable
- selfish
- cry easily
- generally on a short fuse - quick to explode!

Of course any child (or adult) will react with immature emotions when under stress. A child with delayed emotional development will behave in this way all the time, even when there is no obvious stress around.

All children are naturally emotionally immature, but some take longer to develop their emotions than others. There are several different reasons why this might occur:

- as part of generally slow development
- as a personality characteristic
- due to lack of training in emotional control
- due to lack of emotional security.

There is a group of temperamental characteristics that are present at birth which have been shown to be associated with immature emotions. Here are the three main temperamental characteristics:

1. very strong and intense emotional reactions
2. reluctance/slowness in adapting to change
3. unpredictable behaviour and daily habits.

This type of personality tends to continue as the child grows up and it is linked with a higher rate of difficult behaviour than normal. There is good evidence that children who are easily upset and who could be described as emotionally sensitive have a strong tendency to continue to be like that. In fact there is also evidence that the way children react emotionally is to a significant extent inherited. However, the way children manage to cope with their emotions is something that they learn as they grow up.

HOW TO ENCOURAGE EMOTIONAL MATURITY

Fortunately, the emotions of most children develop naturally along the normal lines without parents having to think much about them. But some children may need help with their immature emotions for the following reasons:

- their general development is slow
- they have a 'highly strung' personality
- there has been a lack of training in emotional control

- they have experienced emotional insecurity.

No child will be able to mature properly without a feeling of emotional security, which requires the following type of care:

- a loving and affectionate atmosphere
- predictability of care and relationships
- consistent discipline and limit-setting
- age-appropriate expectations.

If your child is emotionally immature, it is important not to take any of these requirements for granted. None of them is easy to achieve and immature children need them even more than mature children do. It would be a waste of time and effort to try and help emotional development if one or more of these needs is unmet.

   Assuming that everything has been done to provide emotional security for the child, then here are some ideas for what you can do in addition to help your child gain more emotional control:

- Tell your child what sort of emotional control you expect.
- Encourage gradually increasing responsibility.
- Ignore and avoid responding to emotionally immature behaviour.
- Make sure that you and other adults at home set a good example.
- Make a fuss and praise any mature expressions of emotion.
- Try training your child in emotional control.

There are many different ways of training the emotions and exactly how you tackle it will depend on your particular circumstances, but here are some guidelines for training your child to develop more mature emotions:

- Teach which emotion is which by talking about them at every opportunity so that your child can put a name to each feeling.

- Explain how you control your own emotions and demonstrate how it can be done in real life.
- Short training sessions for coping with frustration may help. Choose a situation that you know will cause frustration for your child. Warn him or her about what you are doing and how you would like him or her to react. Give praise and reward for success. For failure – just keep repeating the process until you are successful.
- If your child has shown immature emotions, talk it over some time later and work out together how the emotions could have been managed better.

CONCLUSION

At first it is hard to tell the difference between one emotion and another, but gradually each emotion develops its own special characteristic. Many feelings are made up from a mixture of emotions which makes them complicated to understand and difficult to cope with, but there are several ways of helping your child's emotions to develop well.

5
. . . . .

Wetting and Messing

BLADDER CONTROL

Children begin to have some bladder control by 18 months and are mostly dry by day at two years old. By three years old the majority of children are also dry by night; however about one in three at this age has occasional wetting accidents. By five years old one child in 10 is still wet at night at least once a week.

If wetting continues after the age of four years, there is a good chance that it will carry on for some time, since only about 10 per cent of these children become dry during each subsequent year. Even at the relatively mature age of 10 years old, one in 20 children is still occasionally wet at night and up to 1 per cent of children continue to have occasional wetting accidents into adult life.

Girls tend to become dry earlier than boys, but up to five years old there is little difference in the frequency of wetting between the sexes. After this time the ratio of boys to girls steadily increases so that it is at least five times more common in older boys.

ENURESIS

Because wetting accidents are so common in young children, it isn't considered a problem until a child has reached five years old. It is then called *enuresis*.

Mistaken ideas about why children wet themselves are common and it seems that this has always been the case. Treatments from the past include hedgehog testicle, clamps, boiled mice, standing over a bird's nest while it burns and even strychnine! These desperate remedies show just how frustrated parents can become with their wetting child.

Wetting during the daytime is less common than while asleep during the night – about 15 per cent of enuretic children wet during the day. Sometimes children start to wet for the first time after having been dry for several years; this is called secondary enuresis to distinguish it from wetting that has continued without a break, which is called primary enuresis. In fact there is little evidence that primary, secondary, daytime or night-time wetting are very different from each other. They share much the same characteristics and respond to the same type of treatment.

Myths About Enuresis

Enuresis continues to be misunderstood and to cause distress and confusion for children and parents alike. The myths about enuresis are potentially damaging, because they result in inappropriate treatments and a lack of awareness of the simple and effective treatment options that now exist. Here are the most frequent myths:

- 'There is no need to worry – children grow out of it.'
  Most children do indeed grow out of it, but about 1 per cent don't and long-standing enuresis may leave behind a damaged self-image and a deep sense of failure.
- 'Enuresis is caused by early or forced toilet-training.'
  There is no evidence that early training delays bladder control, in fact quite the reverse. It may well be that delayed toilet-training makes it more difficult for some children to gain continence.
- 'Bedwetting is due to deep sleep.'
  Deep sleep is commonly put forward as an explanation for bedwetting. It has the advantage of absolving both the child and the parent from any blame or responsibility for the enuresis, but

lacks any evidence to support it. Sleep electro-encephalographs have shown that enuresis can occur at any stage of sleep.

- 'Children with enuresis have small bladders.'

The average amount of urine passed on each occasion is about 80 ml at two years of age, increasing to around 225 ml between seven and eight years old. In adults the first sensation of bladder fullness occurs at 150 to 200 ml and the bladder reaches its capacity between 350 and 500 ml. In young children the bladder muscle contracts at relatively low volumes, which results in a rise in bladder pressure and an urge to pass urine. It has been shown that enuretic children pass smaller amounts of urine during the day than children who are dry and produce more urine during the night, but bladder capacity is the same and the total output per 24 hours is also the same.

- 'Enuresis is a symptom of emotional disturbance.'

Although wetting is frequently worse when a child is emotionally distressed, enuresis behaves in much the same way as other conditions such as asthma, nail-biting, and toothache – they all get worse if a child is distressed. If emotional disturbance is the main cause of enuresis then it should respond to the usual treatments for distress such as psychotherapy. However, there is no evidence to support this although the child may continue to wet more happily after psychotherapy.

Symptomatic treatment that is aimed only at stopping the wetting should in theory either be ineffective or result in new symptoms of emotional disturbance. In fact this doesn't happen. Children who become dry as a result of bladder-training flourish and mature.

- 'Enuresis can be treated by "lifting" and fluid restriction.'

Stopping all evening drinks will reduce the extent of wetting but won't stop it. And in the same way, lifting children and putting them on the toilet during the night may well reduce the frequency of wetting but it doesn't stop it. It may even continue for longer because the children come to rely on their parents and forget to take responsibility for bladder control.

What Causes Enuresis?

There is a strong link between accidental wetting and stress factors such as a broken home or poverty. However, this link is most probably an indirect effect due to parents being under stress and therefore being unable to give enough attention to toilet-training – rather than being due to a direct effect of the stress on the child. There is good evidence that if toilet-training is left to look after itself, wetting problems are more likely to occur.

The majority of children with enuresis have a close relative who has or had the same problem. It has been calculated that if a parent has been enuretic as a child there is a 40 per cent chance of his or her child being affected. With identical twins there is a 70 per cent chance of wetting problems in one twin if the other is enuretic. These findings suggest that difficulties with bladder control are quite strongly inherited.

Although the popular view is that wetting is caused by psychological stress, it is more likely that it is actually the other way round, so that it is the enuresis that causes children to become upset and distressed. However, there is evidence that bedwetting is more likely to occur in children who have been unsettled between the age of two and five years, for example by going into hospital or by the birth of a sibling. But this again is most likely to be due to interference with toilet-training combined with immature bladder control.

Enuresis has the characteristics of a specific developmental delay, as has been described in Chapter 3. The evidence for this is that enuresis:

- occurs more frequently in males
- tends to be more of a problem if it occurs in girls
- runs in families
- is associated with other specific delays
- is made worse by stress
- causes secondary emotional distress

- improves with time
- passes through normal maturational stages
- responds to specific training techniques
- doesn't respond to non-training therapies.

This supports the idea that wetting is due to immaturity of the nerve supply and of the co-ordination of the bladder muscles. This immaturity, which is probably inherited, then interacts with other factors such as toilet-training problems and life stresses and results in delayed bladder control.

Any theory about the cause of wetting has to explain why most children manage to gain bladder control without problems. A delay in bladder development seems to fit the facts best. Bladder immaturity is also the best explanation for the wetting that occurs after a period of a year or two of being dry. This secondary enuresis may occur after some form of stressful event. However, the associated characteristics are just the same as those for other specific developmental delays listed above, and the response to treatment is the same.

In about 5 per cent of children who wet it is possible to find an obvious physical reason such as a urine infection or a major physical abnormality of the bladder. In this case the wetting is:

- more likely to occur during the daytime as well as at night
- more likely to occur in girls
- associated with passing urine frequently
- associated with other evidence of bladder problems, such as pain on passing urine, smelly urine or having to rush to the toilet.

Why Bother About Wetting?

Most children who wet themselves eventually become dry, so why bother to do anything about it? Parents are often told 'Whatever you do, don't worry, they will grow out of it – try and make as little fuss about it as possible.' This advice is now out of date and not very helpful for the following reasons:

- If enuresis continues after six to seven years old, it is easy for children to become despondent about ever getting dry.
- Children who wet are often smelly and get teased.
- It is difficult to grow up while still wetting.
- Older enuretic children easily develop a sense of failure.
- Children who have failed in their efforts to become dry may give up trying to succeed in anything and this may affect school work.
- Trips away from home can be made more difficult by the problem.
- A very few children don't grow out of it.
- Doing nothing will keep the problem going for longer.

WHAT CAN BE DONE TO HELP?

Each individual child needs a specially designed treatment plan, and like so many aspects of childcare this is more of an art form than a process that can be rigidly applied. Some of the main issues that need to be considered are outlined below.

Deal with Any Stress

Before embarking upon a bladder-training programme, it is important to consider whether or not there are any obvious stress factors that may be making the wetting worse. These stresses might be physical - such as a structural abnormality of the bladder or an infection of the urinary tract - or they might be psychological. Many stress factors such as the birth of a sibling or moving house can't be easily avoided or easily changed, but other stressful life experiences can be sorted out as far as possible

Distress that is secondary to the enuresis must also be considered. Teasing at school or home and other negative experiences caused by the wetting should be stopped firmly and immediately.

Some children will be in a situation where it is impossible to change the life stresses, such as an illness or family breakdown.

70

However, this doesn't mean that treatment for enuresis is a waste of time – it just means that treatment will need to take into account these background factors.

Improve Motivation and Self-esteem

Many enuretic children have experienced repeated failure in gaining bladder control. It isn't surprising that they easily develop a feeling of failure and lose any motivation to get dry. Before long, feelings of hopelessness and resignation about the incontinence develop. It is also easy for parents to become resigned to wet beds and to take as little notice of the problem as possible.

Everyone needs to keep the motivation going for as long as possible and to do everything to build up the child's self-esteem (see page 120). At the same time, it may sometimes help to have a complete break from trying to get dry. It is probably better to concentrate on intensive bladder-training for a few weeks rather than drifting on in a half-hearted way for months on end.

Encourage Responsibility and Mature Behaviour Generally

Failing to become dry in spite of trying makes children feel like giving up any responsibility for their own wetting and leaving others to clear up the mess. It is all too easy to go along with this in the hope that it will avoid any distress. Unfortunately, doing everything for your child is likely to maintain the wetting and the associated immaturity.

Children should be expected to take some responsibility for wetting accidents and clear up their own mess with whatever help and supervision are necessary for the level of development that they have reached. This is not a punishment but a normal reaction – in the same way that most parents would expect children to clear up milk they have spilt.

Taking responsibility for wetting accidents will mean changing wet sheets or pants and helping to wash them out as well. Even children as young as six years old can be involved in this, provided they are given the help they need.

Parents must take overall responsibility for ensuring that any treatment is carried out correctly. Any scope for mature and responsible behaviour in other areas should be actively encouraged. For example, taking some responsibility around the home or for helping other people.

Medicine

There are several drugs that have been shown to help reduce wetting. None of them is much more than 80 per cent successful and most children start wetting again when the drug is stopped. On the whole they are best avoided because none is free from side-effects and they all take away from the child any feeling of mastery over the problem.

Occasionally it is justified for a child to take medication for enuresis to cover a short period such as a holiday. The drug that is in favour at the moment is related to a hormone, desmopressin, that is released by the brain to reduce the production of urine. It can be taken in the form of snuff, so it certainly has novelty value.

Caffeine is a drug that stimulates the output of urine. It may be worth trying to avoid giving an enuretic child cola drinks, and certainly no coffee or tea, although this may not make any difference.

Bladder-Training is Best

There are many different ways of training the bladder, but the main idea is to make a strong connection between what is happening to the bladder and what the child is thinking. Here are some ideas to try:

Record-keeping

A simple chart or diary that records progress can increase children's awareness of their improvement in becoming dry. It may also help to show if there is a pattern, for example that the enuresis only occurs on certain occasions. A reward chart that uses stars or smiley faces for dry periods can be especially helpful and may even help a child to be dry without having to use any other method.

Bladder Exercises

Bladder exercises on their own have not been shown to be very helpful and shouldn't be used if there is any evidence of a physical problem with the bladder such as an infection. However, they may be useful when combined with other treatments. They have the advantage that they encourage children to feel that they can control their bladder. There are three main exercises, all of which can be enhanced by giving your child a drink beforehand:

1. *Increasing bladder capacity*
   Urine is collected and measured with the aim of improving on the previous record for the largest amount passed in a single pee.
2. *Delaying passing urine*
   When the urge to pee occurs the child goes to the toilet but tries to delay peeing for a gradually increasing period, starting with a delay of a few seconds only and building up by a few seconds at a time in an attempt to beat the previous record.
3. *Stopping and starting*
   Stopping the flow of urine when peeing may be helpful for older children who have some bladder control. It should give a child a sense of mastery over his or her bladder.

The Enuretic Alarm

The wetting alarm is a battery-powered electrical gadget that makes a buzzing sound if a child is wet. There are two main types, but both work on the principle that urine will conduct electricity. In one case a low-voltage electric current is conducted between two metal and gauze pads placed under the bed sheets. In the other type of alarm the current passes between contacts on a small electrode placed in a pad in the front of the pants. If care is taken and persistence used to make sure that the system is working properly then an improvement can be expected in up to 80 per cent of children. (For further details contact the Enuresis Resource and Information Centre [ERIC]), 65 St Michael's Hill, Bristol BS2 8DZ, tel. 0202 556920.)

Unlearning the Habit

Any behaviour that is frequently repeated can easily become a habit. Enuresis is no exception and techniques that disrupt learned habit patterns may be helpful. Changing any part of the bedtime routine or sleeping arrangements (e.g. position of the bed, type of bedclothes, etc.) is worth trying.

Overlearning

This approach is less well known but can be very effective, especially when combined with the buzzer alarm. Overlearning involves excessive repetition of the behaviour to be learned. For enuresis it involves repeated visits to the toilet. The so-called 'dry bed method' (see below) involves 20 visits to the toilet before going to sleep!

The Dry Bed Method

This overlearning approach has been shown to be up to 90 per cent successful within six weeks, which is a very high success rate. But it's hard work!

On the first night the child practises getting out of bed and going to the toilet 20 times, counting up to 20 in bed and in the toilet each time. During the first night the child is woken every hour, given a drink and asked if he or she wishes to go to the toilet. If the child goes to the toilet this is rewarded with praise. If, on the other hand, the child has an accident and wets the bed, the

20-times routine has to be repeated and the child then deals with the wet sheets and puts dry ones on the bed. The whole of this first night obviously has to be closely supervised by the parents. Well, it's only one night!

The following nights are not so demanding. The buzzer alarm is used to signal when the child has wet the bed. Before going to bed the child is encouraged to drink normally. As soon as the buzzer sounds the child gets up and goes to the toilet, changes the sheets and returns to bed. If the child has wet the bed on the night before then the 20-times routine has to be carried out before going to sleep. If the child has been dry then the child can go straight to sleep.

A record is kept each morning of what happened the night before. As soon as there have been seven dry nights in a row the buzzer can be removed. But if the child wets for two consecutive nights at any time in the future, the buzzer is returned to use and the 20-times routine used again in the same way as before. This is all a lot of hassle and it requires the full co-operation of everyone concerned, but it should be worth it. If the child isn't dry or at least much less wet within six weeks, it may be best to have a rest from it for a while and try again in a few weeks' time.

DELIBERATE WETTING

Wetting on purpose is fortunately rare. It can be a worrying sign if it occurs without any obvious cause. If a child deliberately wets either during the day or the night it is usually an indication of distress and emotional upset that needs expert help.

It is not unusual for parents mistakenly to believe that their child is wetting the bed deliberately, but this is not usually the case. Here are some of the reasons why it may seem that a child is wetting the bed on purpose:

- **Wetting may occur soon after being woken up.**
  One of the most common times for wetting is in light sleep, just as a child is waking up. It is likely that the child drifted off to sleep again after first waking and then wet during light sleep before finally waking up fully.
- **Children are often dry when staying away from home.**
  Although this may be due partly to an increased motivation to remain dry, the main reason is likely to be the result of an altered sleep pattern that disrupts the normal habit. The child obviously has no control over this.
- **Some children can go for weeks without a wet bed and then start wetting again.**
  Usually there is an obvious stress that has caused the relapse, but less obvious stresses such as tiredness, excitement or a mild cold may also cause wetting to occur in a child who already has an immature bladder.

You can see that there is usually an explanation for wetting which is outside the child's control. It is therefore important to avoid blaming children for their wetting accidents; being angry will usually make things worse. The best way of reacting to these wetting accidents is to be sad rather than cross and say something like: 'Oh dear, what a shame, better luck next time!' Sometimes parents are told to ignore wetting. This is not only difficult (if not impossible) to do but probably allows enuretic children to believe that they can carry on quietly wetting without bothering about it.

DAYTIME WETTING

Day-wetting is less common than night-wetting, but it occurs more often in enuretic girls than boys. About 15 per cent of enuretic children wet during the day as well as the night and a few wet only during the day. Daytime wetting is more likely to be associated with a physical problem involving the bladder or kidneys, so the child needs to be given a careful physical check-over by your family doctor.

Treatment is really very similar to the normal process of toilet-training a younger child. The main aim is to keep the child dry by going to the toilet frequently enough - at regular intervals by the clock and at any other time if the urge is there. Here are some ideas that might be helpful:

- Use some form of timing device with an alarm. Otherwise it is very easy for your child to forget to go to the toilet.
- The intervals between going to the toilet need to be as short as is necessary to keep your child dry. Maybe once every hour will be necessary at first, or even more frequently.
- Keep a record of when the wetting accidents occur. In this way you may find that the wetting only happens at a particular time. Toileting then needs to be more frequent around this 'at risk' time.
- Concentrate on getting your child to go to the toilet regularly before being concerned about getting dry. If your child won't go to the toilet when expected to, you can hardly be surprised if there are wetting accidents.
- As the child becomes dry, the periods between going to the toilet can be extended.

There are few differences between day- and night-wetting. The main causes are much the same and they both respond to a training approach. The small buzzer alarm can also be used to signal wetting accidents during the day when the child is up and about at home.

SOILING OR MESSING

Soiling - messing pants - sometimes called *encopresis* is similar to wetting in many ways. They are both due primarily to developmental immaturity, occur more frequently in boys and they both respond to training methods of treatment. However, soiling is such an unpleasant thing to cope with that it quickly causes strong feelings in everyone concerned. This makes the relationship between soiling and the emotions much closer than it is with wetting.

In addition to specific developmental immaturity, there are several physical causes that can start soiling off:

- Constipation. This is a frequent cause of soiling and should be treated with a change in diet, with increased fibre, fruit, fluids and also increased exercise. If this fails, mild laxatives or even enemas will be necessary.
- Diarrhoea. A soiling accident when a child has diarrhoea can cause an emotional reaction in the child or the parent. The resulting anxiety may then make repeated soiling more likely.
- Retention. Children sometimes hold back faeces if they think that passing a motion will result in pain or difficulty. The bowel then becomes full of soft faeces but it never gets cleared out. The bowel wall becomes abnormal and stops functioning properly.
- Anal fissure. This is a little split in the skin of the anus usually caused by passing a large motion. This makes it painful for the child to go to the toilet and soon results in retention of faeces and constipation, which in turn may cause soiling.
- Abnormal bowel wall. There are several quite rare conditions that cause the bowel wall to malfunction. Special medical investigations are necessary to detect the abnormality. One of the best indicators for this type of problem is that the bowel disorder can be expected to be present from birth.
- Physical interference. This is an unusual cause of soiling, but it needs to be considered if the soiling continues in spite of treatment. The interference might be carried out by the child or by someone abusing the child.

Once a child has started to soil for whatever reason, the soiling is likely to continue and to develop into a habit. The strong feelings that soiling provokes quickly feed into a vicious circle. However, in the early stages it may be enough simply to treat the underlying physical cause of soiling. For those children who continue to soil, here are some guidelines to follow:

- Have your child sit on the toilet regularly and frequently enough to stay clean. This may mean between four and eight times daily at first. ·
- The first stage is to make sitting on the toilet into an automatic and regular habit that occurs with little or no fuss.
- Insist that the child sit on the toilet for three to four minutes. Put a clock in the toilet for timing the sitting or, even better, use an egg timer!
- A star chart may help – first for sitting regularly on the toilet and then for being clean.
- Make sure that your child's bowel is kept as empty as possible, either by using a very high-fibre diet or using mild laxatives. Any child with constipation or with a loaded bowel has little chance of ever getting clean.
- Children who have soiled should wash out their own dirty pants – not as a punishment but as a way of helping them to be more aware of the problem and more keen to stop it. Children who soil find it so distressing that they quickly learn to shut their minds off from it which doesn't help.
- Lots and lots of praise for success will help avoid the natural feelings of failure and low self-esteem that children who soil easily develop.
- If the messing continues in spite of everything, it usually responds to special small enemas, to be given every evening unless the child has been clean and has also passed a motion during the previous 24 hours. You might think that this would be distressing for any child. At least it is effective and should cause much less disturbance than the soiling does.

Soiling is such a devastating problem for any child to have that after the age of four years it should be treated very vigorously in order to avoid serious emotional consequences. Untreated soiling leads very quickly to all the secondary emotional complications of a poor self-image. Don't wait too long before asking for specialist help from your family doctor.

CONCLUSION

Problems with wetting and messing are largely based on delayed development of the bladder and bowel. Like other developmental disorders they are more common in boys and are made worse by stress, but they respond well to treatment that is based on training. If left untreated, children with enuresis or encopresis may easily develop low self-esteem and feelings of failure. It is therefore not good enough to say 'Don't worry, he'll grow out of it.' Persistent wetting or soiling problems need to be dealt with by a specialist; if this fails or there are emotional complications a referral to a child psychiatrist should be considered.

6

. . . . .

Language – Reading and Writing

EARLY LANGUAGE DEVELOPMENT

It is obvious that children are able to understand quite a lot of what is going on around them and are good at communicating their needs, even before they are able to say a single word. Babies cry or scream to get what they want, while toddlers will point or pull their parents towards whatever it is that they would like to have. These are the first outward signs of language and thought.

By six to eight months old babies begin to make pre-talking sounds called 'babble'. Not long after the babbling starts, children begin to imitate – for example waving 'bye-bye' and copying games. Before children reach a year old there should be signs of understanding simple instructions and gestures such as 'come here' or 'give it to me.'

Between 12 and 18 months the babble gradually develops into recognizable words. Children put sounds together, first by repeating the same sound: 'da da da da da' and then by putting different sounds together: 'mu mi mu mi', copying what they have heard. Deaf children start to babble but don't go on to put sounds together because they can't hear anything to imitate.

An important stage of language development can be seen in the way children use their imagination in play, for example making things out of bricks or playing with dolls as if they were real little people. Imaginary play is the outward sign of 'inner' language. Deaf children develop imaginary play in the normal way but children with language delay will also be slow to learn to play imaginatively.

By two years old most children can produce about 200 words and make short sentences of two to three words. Three-year-old children use as many as 1000 words and become quite creative in the way they use grammar. They know the main rules of grammar but not the exceptions and this often results in children making amusing mistakes. For example, our three-year-old daughter once said 'Where me are you?' meaning, 'Do you know where I am?'

It seems likely that all the different languages in the world have the same underlying structure. English-speaking children may sound very different from Russian or Chinese children, but the actual construction of the languages is very similar. By five years old most children around the world use the main rules of their language's grammar correctly and can make themselves well understood.

DELAYED LANGUAGE

About one in 20 children develops language so slowly that there is cause for concern. If by two years old there is little sign of communication by speaking, a specialist assessment is required. However, if there is a good ability to use sign language for communication and if non-speaking children obviously understand what is being said to them, they may suddenly start talking within a few weeks or months.

Other children who are slow to learn to speak may be generally delayed in other areas of development as well. But children who show no signs of speaking by 18 months old and yet are developing normally in other ways may have a specific difficulty with language (see Chapter 3). There are several possible causes that must be considered when analysing a specific delay in learning to talk:

- deafness
- speech impediment
- lack of language stimulation

- specific language disorder
- a form of childhood autism
- general developmental delay.

It is important to rule out deafness in any child with delayed language. Parents are often better able to tell if their child is deaf than can be assessed by routine testing. So if you are at all concerned that your child may be deaf it is best to ask your doctor for the opinion of a specialist.

Deaf children develop their own 'inner' language in their head, as can be seen by the way they use sign language and gestures to communicate with and by the way in which they play imaginatively with toys. However, there is some evidence that if children are unable to hear they may have problems understanding more abstract concepts.

At five years old about 10 per cent of children still have difficulty making themselves understood because their speech is so unclear due to poor co-ordination of the muscles of speech production. This is not usually associated with a language problem (understanding and using words) and generally improves with time, but sometimes it persists as an immaturity even into adult life. A lisp is a good example of this.

A lack of language stimulation may delay its development, but the deprivation would have to be very extreme to have any significant effect. There are rare cases of children who have been isolated from people for several years. Many of these children have problems with language development later on, but how much of this is due to the lack of language exposure and how much to the fact that the children were originally abnormal, isn't known.

Specific language disorder, like all other specific delays in development, is more common in boys. It may affect different aspects of language, as follows:

- Expressive difficulty – children can understand what is said to them but it is difficult for them to put words together to make any sense.
- Receptive difficulty – children find it difficult to understand what is said to them, although they can make themselves understood quite easily.
- Central difficulty – children show by their non-language skills that they have a good ability, but in spite of this they have difficulty communicating with others as well as understanding what is said to them.

Children with a specific language difficulty can be a puzzle to their parents and to others. The children may appear quite normal to look at, but give the impression that they are in another world or that they have a small but vital bit of their brain missing. They frequently show some of the following signs:

- a tendency to be withdrawn
- an unusual way of speaking
- a dislike of change
- odd mannerisms
- habits and rituals
- obsessions
- having few friends
- exhibiting inappropriate social behaviour
- becoming easily frustrated
- possessing some areas of relative ability.

Perhaps the best way of understanding what it is like to suffer from specific language disorder is to imagine what it would be like to live in a country where you couldn't speak the language and where gestures had a different meaning from usual. The list above describes how many of us would behave in a world where we couldn't understand the language. Fortunately, specific language delay improves as children grow older and can be helped by special language training.

Childhood Autism

Childhood autism is a rare condition affecting roughly one in 2000 children, but autistic features are more frequent and occur in about one in 500 children. About one in every two children with severe learning difficulties can be expected to have some signs of autism.

The main problem in autism is a profound difficulty with language and understanding abstract concepts. It is therefore not surprising that the signs of autism are much the same (only they are more marked) as those for specific language disorder given in the list above. All children with autism have problems with social relationships, which is probably the result of the extreme language difficulty. This results in children not being able to grasp the more subtle aspects of communication that are essential for relationships to flourish.

No single cause has been found for specific language disorder or childhood autism, but it is known that they both occur three times more commonly in boys than girls and that about 15 per cent of affected children have a family history of someone with a similar condition. There is evidence that the disorders of language are linked with problems in brain functioning because there are associated problems, such as difficulty in co-ordination.

Both autism and specific language disorder need to be assessed and treatment organized by specialists in the field of child development and education. It is important that if your child has either condition you insist that it is properly explained in a way that you can understand. This should make it much easier to know how to respond to a child who otherwise can seem very odd.

LEARNING TO READ

The process of putting sounds and symbols together to make meaning is the basis of both language and of reading. The development of reading is therefore very similar to the development of language. This means that any child with delayed development of language skills, for whatever reason, is also likely to have reading problems.

Each letter and printed word is a symbol that is linked with a particular sound or group of sounds. It is the sequence of letters and words that provides the meaning. This means that any child who has difficulty with putting things in an order or sequence is likely to have reading problems. To be able to read, children have to learn that certain letter combinations make up words, each of which has its own sound and meaning. For example, when reading a book:

$$C + A + T = CAT$$
$$Cat + Sat + On + Mat$$

If they get the sequence wrong it makes life very difficult! For example, reversing the sequence of the word 'on' produces:

cat sat NO mat

and changing the word order results in:

mat sat on cat

When children start to read books they are more interested in the pictures than the words at first. In fact, pictures are themselves a form of language in that they are symbols of the real thing. Picture books are therefore very helpful in preparing children for reading.

Most children make a start with reading well before they go to school. Pre-reading skills include the following abilities:

- to sit still and concentrate for a few minutes
- to recognize the different shapes of letters and/or words
- to make a link between letters, words, sounds and meaning
- to realize that the sequence of letters and words is crucial.

Reasonably good eyesight is obviously necessary for reading. However, even children with very poor vision usually manage to read at the usual age. Provided that children have been able to look at books and have them read to them, most will have made a start towards reading by five years old. The majority of children only have to sit beside someone reading a simple book and pointing to each word as it is read aloud – and hey presto, they can read!

How children learn to read is not well understood and there have been many different theories that have led to the claim that one method of teaching is better than another. But it seems that most children would learn to read even if they had no formal teaching at all. Unfortunately about 20 per cent of children find learning to read quite difficult.

By eight years of age most children have learned the basics of reading and have reached the stage where all that is necessary is for them to practise and to learn to become more fluent and to speed up. When children have reached the reading age of a nine year old they are regarded as being literate, although the World Health Organization sets the age level of literacy at 12 years.

Specific Reading Difficulty or Dyslexia

Dyslexia is a word that produces strong feelings, partly because people misuse it so that it often means something different to each person. The word *dyslexia* makes it sound as though there is a single understandable explanation for a child's not being able to read, which is very rarely the case. More often than not there are several different factors working together.

Although there is still dispute about what exactly constitutes dyslexia, specific reading difficulty is recognized by education authorities as a condition that causes problems with learning to read and which may require specialized teaching. Dyslexia is also recognized as both a medical and a developmental disorder. However, because the word dyslexia (Greek for 'difficulty with words') so easily leads to confusion and disagreement, it is best avoided. There are suitable alternatives that have much the same meaning, such as:

- specific reading disorder
- specific learning difficulty
- specific developmental delay in reading.

It is the specificity of the reading problem that is the most important finding. This distinguishes it from reading problems due to general developmental delay - which affects all areas of development - and from reading problems - which are due to a lack of opportunities to read or to poor teaching.

A gap of two years between the expected reading age for a child's mental ability and his or her actual reading level is considered to be significant enough to be called specific reading delay. So, for example, a child with a mental age of 10 years who is reading at an eight year old's level or less would be regarded as having a significant problem.

This means that because reading starts at five years it isn't possible to identify specific reading delay until a child is seven years old, which may seem rather late. However, there are a number of factors that are frequently found to be linked with specific reading problems; if a child has any of these there is an increased risk of developing specific reading delay:

- muscle co-ordination problems
- confusion between left and right
- sequencing problems
- visual perception difficulties
- other specific delays
- letter and word reversals
- short-term memory problems.

There is no single factor that is known for certain to cause specific reading problems. However, all the features of specific developmental problems are associated:

- Males are more often affected than females (4:1).
- There is a family history of similar difficulties in 20 per cent of cases.
- Other specific delays are frequently associated with reading delay.
- The problems respond to appropriate teaching.
- The problems are made worse by stress and by distress.

Because there is no single cause for specific reading problems, many people have been able to think up all kinds of amazing explanations for why some children are unexpectedly slow to learn to read. So far none of them has been proved in spite of many claims to the contrary. Whatever you are told by experts needs to be taken with a pinch of salt until most of them are saying the same thing – and that hasn't happened yet!

All these theories about reading problems have led to different methods of treatment, many of which have been shown to work well. The treatment approaches that have produced results have the following characteristics:

- individualize the approach
- use standard good teaching methods
- increase self-confidence and enjoyment of the written word
- deal with anxiety about reading
- provide practice for any weak areas
- use encouragement and praise.

With the appropriate help children can be expected gradually to improve their reading, although there is always a risk that they will become disheartened and give up if they don't have enough individual help. There is a lot that you can do at home to help your child with reading problems. Here are some ideas:

- Read to your child with him or her sitting by your side.
- Whatever you do, keep it good fun.
- Keep the sessions short. Five or 10 minutes is enough.
- Use the time for reading practice and enjoyment.
- If you feel bored, the chances are that your child does, too.
- Think up some reading and spelling games for extra fun.
- Additional rewards and incentives may be necessary.
- Don't try and teach, that is what teachers are for.
- Don't give up reading to your child until he or she can read well.

Keep a look-out for a sense of failure developing. It happens so easily because success at school depends so much on being able to read well. Fortunately, feelings of failure don't usually develop much before seven years old. But once a sense of failure has developed it can be difficult to put right and may lead to your child opting out of school.

SPELLING

Spelling is also closely related to language development in that a particular combination of symbols (letters) are put together in a way that gives them meaning. Spelling skills develop after children have learned to read. But the process of learning to spell takes a long time and often goes on into adult life. At least one in five children has significant difficulties with spelling.

Most of the characteristics associated with specific reading delay are also linked with spelling problems. An interesting finding is that the inheritance factor in spelling problems is stronger than for reading difficulty and may account for up to 50 per cent of cases.

Helping a child to spell correctly is much more difficult than helping with reading, but much the same approach should be beneficial. Spelling games in particular are a good way to keep things from getting too serious. Tears and tension about spelling or reading need to be avoided at all costs.

CONCLUSION

Language development is very complicated but is vital for communicating and forming relationships. Reading and spelling are based on language and form such an important part of schooling that any child with language, reading or spelling problems is going to be seriously disadvantaged at school. Although all language problems tend to improve with time and practice, the risks of developing a sense of failure are too great to do nothing. Specialist help and assessment are necessary.

7
. . . . .

Delayed Development

IS MY CHILD DEVELOPING NORMALLY?

It is easy to feel very proud if your child says or does something at an earlier age than expected. Somehow, a child's development is taken as a sign of whether or not the parents are doing a good job, but this isn't the case. Parents can only make a slight difference to a child's rate of development.

It is easier to influence children's development in the first few years of life when the rate of change is so fast. In the long run, however, the main influence that parents have is not so much on the actual level of development, but on how their child's skills are used. For example, children with good hand-eye co-ordination or with a special ability with mathematics are likely to continue to have these skills, but whether or not children take full advantage of them will be influenced by their parents' attitude and support.

The task of a parent is therefore not to achieve the fastest rate of child development nor to have the brightest child in the country. It is to help children make the most of their skills and abilities. No one can ask for more than that.

Hearing the News

Parents are often the first to know that there is a problem with their child's development. This may be just a vague feeling that something is wrong, without knowing exactly what it is. Even so, the news that your child is behind in development is likely to come as a shock.

Explaining the reasons for the delayed development and its implications is a sensitive matter. It is best done gradually, as a continuing process over many weeks so that you as the parent have plenty of time to ask questions and to work out what it all means. Do ask questions - and be prepared to ask for a second opinion.

There are a number of different professionals who might be the first to confirm that your child's development is delayed. The most important thing is that you should trust the person who is breaking the news. If you don't have this trust and confidence in the professional, it is best to try and find someone else with whom you feel more comfortable. At the same time it is important to avoid going from one professional to another just to find somebody who says what you want to hear.

All parents have a picture in their mind of how they would like their children to turn out eventually. Discovering that your child is slow in development will almost certainly mean that you have to change how you see your child and your expectations for the future. This involves losing the image and the hopes that you had that were based on the idea that your child would develop normally. This loss can be similar to a bereavement, with exactly the same normal stages to go through:

1. shock and disbelief
2. acute distress, anger and feelings of guilt
3. gradual acceptance of the situation and learning to cope.

Guilt Feelings

A natural and expected part of being a parent is feeling guilty. We all set out to be wonderful parents, but it doesn't take long to discover that it is impossible to get it right all the time. Parenting is about making compromises and finding a balance between children's demands and parents' needs - since they are often different.

Guilt feelings are so much part of parenting that we develop ways of coping, such as:

- being over-indulgent with food and toys
- giving in to demands
- arranging unnecessary treats
- making allowances for bad behaviour
- blaming oneself or others
- rejecting or over-protective
- being excessively angry or sad.

All these reactions are understandable. We all react in these ways. But guilt is such a destructive emotion that you need to watch out for it and guard against it becoming so powerful that it takes you over.

One of the best ways of dealing with these guilt feelings is to remember that it is impossible to be a perfect parent all the time and to remind yourself constantly about all the things that you have managed to get right. Remember that when things go wrong, you are not alone. Other parents have the same problems too.

Here are some of the ways that parents of disabled children use to cope with their feelings of guilt over the fact that their child is not 'normal':

- concentrating on every positive aspect of the situation
- considering it a privilege to care for a special child
- responding to the challenge of caring for a disabled child
- believing that you have been chosen to take on the special responsibility of a disabled child
- thinking that your child will do better in your family than in another.

INTELLIGENCE AND IQ

Intelligence describes everything to do with the way that we think and solve problems. It is one of the three aspects of the mind:

1. intelligence - thinking
2. emotions - feeling
3. behaviour - willing.

Each mental function is closely connected with the others. For example, it isn't easy to think about something without having feelings about it, and most of the things we do are related to what we are thinking. In spite of this, intelligence is usually measured separately from feelings and behaviour, using tests that are based on questions and tasks in order to assess either verbal skills or practical ability.

Intelligence tests produce a result called the IQ (Intelligence Quotient) that is calculated by dividing the child's mental age by his or her actual age and multiplying by 100. So, for example, a 10-year-old child with a mental age of a five year old will have an IQ of 50.

5 years (mental age) ÷ 10 (actual age) = 0.5
0.5 x 100 = 50 (IQ score)

In young children the result of developmental tests are expressed as a DQ (Development Quotient) instead of IQ because it is the child's general development that is being assessed, but the principle is the same. It is important to know that most IQ tests only go up to the 16-year-old level of ability because people don't become much more intelligent after that age – they just get better at using what ability they do have.

The measurement of intelligence has been criticized because it implies that it is possible to measure the mind with simple tests that have little to do with everyday life. However, the IQ and DQ tests are better than almost any other method of predicting what rate of progress a child will have in the future. Under five years old the tests are not so good at predicting the future, but as children grow older, the tests become increasingly predictive.

Personality is the characteristic way that a person feels and behaves and is rather separate from intelligence. This means that it is possible to have a very bright, intelligent child who has an immature, difficult personality. On the other hand, it is equally possible to have a child with delayed development who has a lovely personality and is a delight to be with in spite of being very behind developmentally.

HOW MANY CHILDREN?

'Slow' development can cover a wide range from just a little delayed to very disabled and there are many terms used to describe such development:

- learning difficulty
- mental handicap
- educational subnormality
- mental deficiency
- developmental delay
- mental retardation.

For practical purposes children with delayed development can be divided into those who are mildly affected and those who are more severely affected in the following way:

1. **mildly delayed development – IQ or DQ of 50 to 70**
   needs extra support and supervision
   will require some special help with schooling
   developmental stages reached noticeably later
   will need some extra help and support as an adult

can be expected to be employable in an unskilled job

may have a family, but will need a supportive partner
2. **moderately or severely delayed development – IQ or DQ
   of less than 50**

   will always require help with many everyday tasks

   development very slow

   needs full time special schooling

   will have significant problems with communication

   will never be able to live independently.

Using these definitions of disability, about 23 children in every 1000 are mildly delayed in development and four children in every 1000 are moderately or severely delayed in development. For specific developmental delay the number of children affected is around 100 in every 1000 children, although this will depend on the age of the child (see Chapter 3).

WHY MY CHILD?

There are so many different causes of slow development that it is often difficult to be sure what the real cause might be. More often than not there is more than one cause for the delay. However, the causes are rather different for mild delay and for severe delay:

MILD DELAY
- 95 per cent have no obvious cause, but lack of stimulation and learning opportunities, as well as possible genetic factors, may play a part. The most likely explanation for most of this group is that it is just the extreme end of the normal range of ability. Some children are fast developers and others are slow in the same way that some are tall and others are short, without anything being wrong with them.
- 3 per cent have slow development that is associated with cerebral palsy.
- 2 per cent have suffered physical damage to the brain.

MODERATE AND SEVERE DELAY

- At least 30 per cent have a chromosome abnormality. Down's syndrome is an example of a chromosome abnormality and is the single most common cause for moderate and severe developmental delay. Fragile X syndrome is another quite common cause.
- 30 per cent have suffered physical damage to the brain.
- 20 per cent have slow development that is associated with cerebral palsy.
- 20 per cent have no obvious cause.

The more delayed the development is, the more likely it is that a definite cause can be found, but it is quite unusual to find a cause where treatment will result in normal development.

All babies are routinely tested shortly after birth to check for the most common conditions that cause delayed development. In addition to this, every child who shows any evidence at all of delayed development should be assessed early on in life by a child development specialist to see if there is a preventable cause that can be dealt with.

SPECIAL PROBLEMS

There are several special problems that are linked with delayed development which make caring for a learning disabled child much more of a heavy responsibility than caring for other children. For example, the more delayed children are in their development, the more likely they are to suffer from:

- deafness and blindness
- challenging behaviour
- growth problems

- co-ordination problems
- communication problems
- birth defects
- psychiatric disorders
- epileptic fits
- social isolation.

These problems are over and above those that are due to delayed development. In addition, the more severe the learning difficulty the wider the gap (or scatter) is likely to be between the different skills and stages of development. For example, a 14-year-old boy might be growing normally and even be tall for his age, but his general development may not have reached that of a seven year old (IQ less than 50) – in addition he might be emotionally even more immature and be functioning more at a four-year-old level with a low tolerance for frustration.

This wide range of functioning, from normal to very delayed, makes it difficult to know how best to respond to a child whose development is delayed.

HELPING YOUR CHILD

It can be very helpful to work out what stage of development your child has reached. You will then have a much better idea about how to react to the delay. This approach has been criticized in the same way that IQs have. It is only a rough estimate and your child may have skills at several different levels all at the same time.

Children with delayed development need to be dealt with in a way that is appropriate for the stage that they have reached. It is no good expecting 10 year olds to be able to read if they are at a two-year-old level of development. Or if a child is still not walking at three years of age, there may be no need to be concerned about this if it is known that the child's developmental stage is so delayed that it is less than that of a one year old.

If your child is generally delayed in development, the first thing to do is to make sure that you are in touch with all the right experts and the best services to help you and your child. Each health district has a slightly different way dealing with this and it also depends on the stage at which it is realized that your child has developmental problems. Every child has a number of routine developmental checks that have to be carried out at different stages. It is unlikely, therefore, that delayed development will be missed, but if you are in any doubt you should ask to see a specialist in child development.

The list of people who might become involved with a child who has developmental delay is enormous. You may find it helpful to use a check-list to help you think about whether or not your child needs extra help from any of the following professionals:

- paediatrician
- health visitor
- family doctor
- social worker
- educational psychologist
- special teacher
- speech therapist
- physiotherapist
- occupational therapist
- community physician (child health)
- community nurse
- clinical psychologist
- child psychiatrist
- other specialist doctors (e.g. for vision, hearing or movement problems)
- voluntary workers.

Each child will have a different pattern of needs for professional skills and special help, so you won't have to deal with all these people. Even so, it may be difficult to keep track of who is doing what.

When your child has started at school it is important for at least one of his or her teachers to take a special interest in your child and be someone you can contact. In addition there should be one person acting as a key worker who knows which professionals are involved and who can make sure that everything necessary is being done to assist you and your child.

It is easy to feel that you are lost in a jungle of different professionals and as a result to feel quite helpless. Here are some ideas that will guard against that happening:

- Make sure that there is at least one professional whom you trust and have some faith in.
- Find out who has some influence over the resources for your child.
- Use this person as your adviser and your guide through the services.
- Don't hesitate to complain if you are not getting all the help you need.
- It may help to have a friend or a parent of a child with similar problems as a supporter/advocate, especially if you are having problems with any of the professionals.

COPING ON YOUR OWN

Caring for a developmentally delayed child is a great responsibility and to do it without outside assistance is difficult to say the least. On the other hand it can sometimes be helpful to be able to work things out for yourself and not be dependent on professional advice all the time. Here are some general guidelines so that you can make your own assessment of your child and to see how that fits in with what you are being told:

- First work out what stage of development your child has reached. You can do this by asking friends or child development experts, or by working it out from the stages of normal development quoted in this book.

- Remember that every aspect of a child's development may not all be at the same level, so you will have to work out an overall average developmental age.
- When you have decided on your child's overall age of development, this will tell you what to expect from the child.
- You can then give all the support and supervision that would be appropriate for a child of that stage of development.
- Watch out for guilt feelings getting in the way and making you do too much for your child and not enough for yourself.
- There are many people - professionals, friends and relatives - who are only too willing to help out. Don't use your child as an excuse for not asking for help.
- Do keep looking after yourself as well as your child. It is easy to forget that you have needs too. In the end it is your child who will lose out if you aren't reasonably rested and relaxed.

So the solution to coping on your own is . . . don't do it. It really is a very great responsibility to care for a child who is severely learning disabled and it is reasonable to share this with other people. The government recognizes this and provides several grants and allowances in recognition of the work that you are doing. The professional worker who is most involved in helping you with your child should be able to tell you how to get information on this.

If you are not sure whom to ask for help, try your child's doctor or teacher. The local social services office should be able to tell you how best to make a request for help. If you are not satisfied, keep asking until you find someone who is able to help you.

SELF-HELP SKILLS

This is the term used to describe all the everyday tasks that we would normally take for granted, such as getting out of bed in the morning and getting washed and dressed. Self-help skills include the following:

- feeding with hands
- drinking from a cup
- eating with a knife, fork and spoon
- managing the toilet
- washing
- cleaning teeth
- undressing and dressing
- making a drink
- cooking a meal.

These self-help skills are really important. It is therefore better to concentrate on training your child to be able to develop as many of these skills as possible than to be too concerned about more academic learning. Being able to do some or all of these things will give children confidence and improve their self-esteem. At the same time the burden of care will be reduced and the children will be more prepared for their future life.

Communication

Children with delayed development will naturally take longer before they can communicate clearly. This may cause problems because they are likely to become active and mobile before they are able to understand instructions or make themselves understood. Outbursts of frustration and temper often stem from communication problems.

Delay in learning to communicate will also result in difficulties in relationships and with further learning. This means that it is important to communicate as clearly as possible with children who are delayed in their development, using every possible method, for example:

- gesture - using fingers, hands and arm movements
- facial expression
- tone of voice
- simple words
- sign language
- drawings and pictures.

There are several different systems of sign language and if your child seems likely to have communication problems that will continue after three to four years of age, it will almost certainly be worth while training your child to use signing. A speech therapist should be able to tell you which system is best to use.

Make sure that you learn and use the sign language at home and don't be put off by those who claim that signing only confuses children and stops them from communicating with words. All the evidence suggests that all forms of communication help in developing language.

HABITS

Because children with delayed development take so long to pass through each stage and on to the next, it is very easy for habits to get stuck. In normal development the habits may occur for a short time, but then fade away when the child moves on to the next stage of development. But if development is delayed, this will take much longer. So it isn't surprising that a particular behaviour becomes stuck.

Look out for bad habits and try and stop them early on (see my book *Good Habits, Bad Habits* in this series). However, there is a positive side to this because the same tendency to become stuck with bad habits can also be used to develop good habits.

SAFETY

Children who develop at a delayed rate will naturally spend longer progressing through each stage. This means that it will be much longer before delayed learning children can be trusted to be safe on their own. Special problems can arise if, for example, a child is functioning at the level of a one year old but is the size and has the mobility of a seven year old. In this case the child will have no idea of common dangers such as heat, heights or traffic but could easily get into dangerous situations unless the supervision is as intensive as that for a much younger child – or even more so.

Work out what level of development your child has reached and this will tell you what level of supervision and protection he or she needs. It is easy to think that because a child with delayed development may be normal in size that he or she should be treated in the same way as other children of that age, but this would be a mistake.

Having worked out your child's stage of development, it is a good idea to go round the house thinking of all the dangers that there might be for a child of that age. It is difficult to make every room child-proof (where your child can be without supervision), but the child's bedroom should be totally safe. Here are some ideas for making things safe:

- Put special safety locks on windows and external doors.
- Screw furniture to the wall if it could be pulled over.
- Use burglar alarms – or lock the doors – if you are concerned about your child wandering into unsafe rooms.
- Repeatedly train your child to know danger and to be safe.

CONCLUSION

Looking after a child with delayed development is a challenge. There are no easy solutions, but in the end the extra responsibility and hard work can be expected to pay off. The aim is to help your child make the most of what ability he or she has and to concentrate on encouraging kindness, caring and warm affection - human qualities that are far more important than being very intelligent or advanced in development.

8

. . . . .

Questions and Answers

Parents usually ask two types of questions when they have been given some advice. 'Yes, but . . .' is what you would say if you were not really convinced about something you have read and you could think of all kinds of reasons why you should not believe it, or if you thought that I had missed something. The other type of question is 'What if . . .?' asked when you want to know more about something.

YES, BUT . . .

It is nonsense to claim that there are any developmental differences between boys and girls

There are interesting differences in the rate of development between boys and girls. Girls are at least one week more mature than boys at birth. Later on this gap increases to one year at the age of eight and two years at puberty.

Boys are generally more vulnerable than girls. Here is some of the evidence:

- most miscarriages are male
- more stillbirths are male
- more boy babies die in the first year of life
- more boys are born disabled
- more boys die in accidents

- all developmental disorders are more common in boys
- males die on average five years earlier than females
- the following conditions are all more common in males:
    reading problems
    bedwetting
    soiling
    language problems
    stammering and stuttering
    clumsiness
    hyperactivity
    psychiatric disorders
    some genetic disorders.

As if to make up for this increased vulnerability of male children, more boys than girls are born. The most likely explanation for these very real differences is that boys have less genetic material in their sex chromosomes than do girls. The two female chromosomes are in the form XX, but male chromosomes can only manage XY, where the missing portion of the X chromosome leaves it in the form of a Y. It is thought that this allows some of the genes on the male X chromosome to be unbalanced. In spite of this simple explanation for the differences between boys and girls, the chances are that it is much more complicated than that.

I think the personality of my child was already determined before birth

You are probably about 80 per cent correct! Children have definite temperamental characteristics at birth. They vary a lot in how passive or active they are and how they react to changes in their environment. Experience with identical twins shows how temperamental characteristics tend to persist in a most remarkable way, even in twins who are separated at birth. The evidence from twin and adoption research suggests that up to 80 per cent of a child's personality is genetically determined.

This doesn't mean that children can never change their personality. The way I look at it, personality is a bit like a picture: at birth the size of the canvas and the colours of the different paints (temperaments) is fixed, but it is the brush strokes of life experience that develop and then complete the picture.

If you think of people you have known for a long time you will realize how little most of them have changed. This also fits in with temperament being largely determined before birth.

I can't understand how a buzzer alarm stops children wetting the bed

No one is quite sure how the enuretic alarm helps children to become dry. In theory it shouldn't work if the alarm sounds only *after* the wetting occurs. However, it may work by interrupting the wetting habit and by making the child feel more involved with the process.

If used correctly the enuretic alarm has up to an 80 per cent success rate. Here are the main factors that seem to be linked with a successful outcome:

- The child must be made responsible for looking after the buzzer, for setting it up and for switching it on and off.
- When the buzzer goes off the child gets up and goes to the toilet to attempt to pass any remaining urine.
- After going to the toilet the child changes the wet pants/sheets and puts them in to soak.
- Finally the buzzer is set up again, just in case there is another wetting accident.
- Parents must supervise and make sure that their child is following the routine properly.
- Using a chart to record progress can be helpful, as can: setting targets to aim for and rewards for reaching them. For example, one dry night is worth a small treat or a few pence. When this has been achieved on one or two occasions, the

target becomes two dry nights in a row and then three and so on for the same reward on each occasion.

avoiding large rewards and making the same reward progressively more difficult to achieve is important, otherwise children quickly learn to work the system for their own benefit!

You haven't said anything about normal toilet-training

Most children will become clean and dry whatever you do, but here are some guidelines which will make it more likely that a child will be toilet-trained easily and quickly.

- You can start toilet-training when your child is old enough to sit safely on the potty without support (around 10 to 12 months old), but don't expect any success at this stage.
- Remember that bowel control isn't expected before 18 months and that children can't be expected to have full control of bowel and bladder before three years old (10 per cent of five year olds and 5 per cent of 10 year olds still have occasional accidents going to the toilet).
- It is best to avoid being too relaxed and unconcerned about toilet-training or your child may not get the message. Also avoid being cross or upset about toileting.
- Start by sitting the child on the potty at every nappy change, to make it a routine and not something that can be argued about. Do the same things each time so that it becomes automatic for your child.
- Expect your child to sit on the potty for long enough to have a chance of producing something. Start with a few seconds only and gradually build up to 30 seconds for a pee and up to three minutes for a poo. Making a child sit on the pot for ages in the hope that something will eventually happen risks the development of resentment and refusal to sit.
- When you feel the time is right, leave the nappies off and keep

the potty close by. At this stage it is helpful to get your child to sit on the toilet more frequently than before - frequently enough to keep him or her clean and dry.

- Although it is important that children feel comfortable and happy sitting on the toilet, giving them a toy or book to read may act as a distraction.
- Any success, either for sitting for the right amount of time or for producing something, needs to be praised to such an extent that your child feels really proud.

My daughter can't manage to do any of the bladder exercises

Most children below five years old are likely to find delaying going to the toilet and stopping and starting difficult. It might also be a problem if there is a physical problem with the bladder or kidneys that may show itself with any of the following symptoms:

- frequent daytime wetting over the age of three years
- discomfort on passing urine
- strong-smelling urine
- constant dribbling of urine
- having to rush frequently to the toilet.

However, in most cases there is little or no sign of any physical abnormality. If in any doubt get a specialist's opinion.

I have been told not to fuss about my eight-year-old son who still wets the bed because he will eventually grow out of it

More than 99 per cent of children do grow out of it. However, there is a serious risk of the child developing emotional problems as a result of the wetting if it continues after the age of seven or eight years. The following problems may occur:

- low self-esteem due to feeling wet and smelly

- poor self-image due to the nasty remarks people make
- a feeling of failure because the child has tried to get dry and in spite of all the efforts has failed
- a tendency to give up easily with anything that is difficult
- a denial of any problem, including the wetting.

It is worth while starting to help children with a wetting problem as soon as it seems to be interfering with their lives. Remember that wetting is almost always a developmental immaturity which the child can't help, so there is no point in getting cross and upset. On the other hand, if you take no notice of the wetting it is especially likely to continue if your child is aged five years or older.

I have been told that bedwetting is a sign of hidden depression or aggression

This view is based on the theories of psychoanalysis but there is no evidence to support it. In fact depressed children are, if anything, less likely to wet. The quick response of some enuretic children to anti-depressant medication has been shown to be unrelated to any effect on depression. The medication has a purely symptomatic effect, and in most cases the wetting starts again when the medicine is stopped.

How can self-confidence be developed?

There are many things that you can do to help develop your child's self-confidence:

- Set up situations where you know that your child will be able to succeed. Start with something that you know can be achieved quite easily and very gradually make the task harder, but never before the previous stage has been successfully attained.
- Protect your child from repeated failures.
- Give extra praise for everyday activities.

- Avoid using negative statements about your child, such as 'You are hopeless,' 'I have no confidence in you,' 'I knew you wouldn't be able to do it.'
- Make sure that you haven't set standards for your child that are too high.
- Show that you have confidence in your child – and say so, too.
- Point out and emphasize every success.
- Tell your friends, in front of your child, how pleased you are with any achievement.
- Deal with any jealousy that your child may have, because this emotion is closely linked with a lack of confidence.
- Make sure that no one is undermining what you are doing, especially other relatives and people at school.
- Consistent loving care and clear discipline will protect your child's self-confidence and lead to the development of a feeling of security.

Everyone tells my that my son's development is slow, but I don't believe them

Well, it depends who it is that is telling you. If it is an expert in child development, then it is wise to believe what you are told. Specialists in child development know only too well how difficult it is to be sure about how a child is progressing and they will therefore be very careful about what they say. However, you can always ask for a second opinion.

One way of assessing how your son is progressing is to observe him with other children to see if his skills and behaviour are about the same as theirs. By about seven to eight years old it is usually obvious what kind of progress a child is making, but don't forget that there is a wide range of ability that can be considered normal and which does not require very special teaching.

I think my daughter is behind in some of her development, but nobody will believe me

Parents are usually very good at judging if their child is behind in development. They often get it right and the experts are eventually proved wrong. Of course there is a danger if you take your child from one person to another until your view is confirmed. Most important is to find a specialist in child development whom you feel you can trust to discuss your concern about your daughter. If you are still not satisfied, ask for a second opinion.

I have been told that we shouldn't speak a different language at home from that spoken at school

Children who are brought up to be bilingual seem to do better than most in the development of their language ability. Even children as young as three years old seem to be able to move from one language to the other with the greatest of ease - without becoming muddled. Children quickly learn which language to use when, and will use whichever language produces the quickest result.

However, children with delayed language development will have additional problems if they are brought up as bilingual. In these cases it is best to decide which language is likely to be the most practical and useful and then to keep to using that one language with the child as much as you can.

I think that the stages of development you give are all too advanced

Don't forget that stages of development are only guidelines and there is a lot of variation from one child to another. It is quite possible for a child to be a bit behind on all the stages of development and still do well in the long run. The real crunch time comes when children start at school, because if they can't keep up with their classmates they will have major problems unless they receive special teaching help.

What can I do to help my daughter who is slow in learning to read?

It is helpful to know if your daughter is generally delayed with most aspects of her development or if it is just the reading that is a problem. If she is generally delayed, she may actually be reading at the expected level for her stage of development. Ask her teacher and if in doubt get specialist advice from an educational psychologist.

Usually it is best to leave teaching to the teachers, with any reading that you do at home to be practice only. Here are some guidelines for practising reading with your child:

- Any reading is better than none, so don't worry too much about whether the reading material is good literature or not.
- Choose a book that your child will find both interesting and quite easy to read.
- Reading with you must be good fun. Think of ways that you can make a game out of it, for example alternating reading between you or using a reward for so many correctly read words.
- Sit together so that you can both see the book at the same time.
- If your daughter finds a word difficult to read it is best to tell her it rather than expecting her to struggle and guess what it could be.
- Encourage reading of anything – for example, packets and signs, or you could write interesting notes for your daughter to read: 'When you have read this you can have a cuddle!'

WHAT IF . . .?

I have been told that my son has Aspergers syndrome

Although there is some dispute about whether Aspergers syndrome is a useful label, it does seem to describe children who are clumsy, socially withdrawn, have odd ritualistic mannerisms and find communication difficult. In many ways these children are very similar to mild cases of autism and it seems likely that the underlying problem is difficulty with abstract language.

Like autism and specific language disorder, the condition is more common in boys. Treatment involves intensive social and language training to improve the weak areas.

My daughter is clumsy – can anything be done about it?

There are several different types of clumsiness and many causes of the problem. Occasionally it is due to brain damage, in which case there will have been an obvious episode when this occurred that you will know about. If there has been no apparent brain injury, then the most likely cause of clumsiness is a specific developmental delay (see page 10).

Clumsiness may affect mainly the large muscles in the trunk and limbs, which would make actions like throwing a ball and running difficult, or it can mainly affect the small muscles in the hand with the result that writing clearly is difficult.

Treatment is by training the muscles to be better co-ordinated. There is nothing magical about this. All that is involved is intensive training – rather like an athlete – at whatever it is that your daughter finds difficult. Make sure that the training is always based on success, otherwise you may find that repeated inability to co-ordinate properly will make her feel a failure.

My son is two years old and has not yet said more than 'mama' and 'dada'

Being slow to talk is not unusual. Remember that 10 per cent of five year olds have difficulty making themselves understood outside the family. Although boys take a little longer to learn to talk than girls, by two years old your child should be making short sentences. Sometimes children are slow to talk if there are other children or relatives who can work out what is meant from their gestures, because they then don't need to speak.

An expert assessment by a specialist in child development is what is needed. It is important to determine if your son is deaf at the earliest possible moment. In addition it will help to know if your son is generally slow in development or if this is a specific problem.

Treatment is much the same whatever the cause, although some causes are easier to help than others. Expert advice is important, but you can help your son by frequently talking with him using simple words only – naming things and using gestures to back up what you are saying. From time to time it helps to check how much your son has understood of what you have just said by asking simple questions. Like reading practice it is important to keep this talking practice good fun.

My four-year-old son is hyperactive

Hyperactivity can be very difficult to cope with, but it isn't done deliberately, as can be seen from the following list of causes:

- Hyperactivity and restlessness is a normal stage of development between the ages of two and six years. In some children, especially boys, this phase can last even longer.
- Distressed children who have had to cope with a lot of family stress tend to be more restless and unsettled.
- Children who have been allowed too much freedom to do as they please are often restless and demanding.
- A few children, especially those with some sort of brain disorder such as epilepsy or birth injury are hyperactive due to a medical condition called either the hyperkinetic syndrome or attention deficit disorder.
- Children who are over-stimulated and overexcited will be hyperactive.
- Lack of sleep can cause children to be overactive.
- Although there is no firm evidence, it is possible that particular foods and additives make children restless.

Hyperactive children benefit not only from dealing with the cause if possible, but also from routine and regularity in everyday life, with firm boundaries set for their behaviour. Concentration exercises can help - you could ask your child to concentrate on a task for a few seconds, timed by the clock and then gradually increase the time over several weeks, always ending each concentration session on a note of success.

My daughter has to go to a school for slow learners

Schools for slow learners are usually better equipped to teach children with learning difficulties, so you can expect your daughter to do better there than at a 'normal' school. The decision about which school is best can be difficult if a child's ability is in the borderline area. In all cases it is best to give what seems to be the right school a trial for a term or two, but to keep a close watch on what progress is being made.

It is especially necessary to form a partnership with your daughter's school so that she can make the most of what it has to offer. It is difficult to decide what schooling is best for any child and there are always advantages and disadvantages to every school. It may help to ask parents of other children at the school what they think about it before you make a final decision.

My daughter has growing pains

Children often complain of aches and pains and if there are no other signs of anything obviously wrong it can be very difficult to know what the cause might be. There is no evidence that normal growth is painful, but there are a few conditions that cause pain as a result of abnormal growth.

Pain may also be caused by a wide range of conditions for which there are no outward signs of abnormality, so it is best to ask your doctor to check your daughter carefully. If nothing is found, it is best not to assume that it must be 'all in the mind'. Physical pain always causes an emotional reaction and emotional distress always results in physical changes such as altered breathing and heart rate.

It is very common for children to have a part of their body where they experience pain when they are upset. The most common places to experience pain are the head, the tummy and the legs. You will easily recognize this after a few occasions.

A pain that is caused by emotional upset is no less painful than if there is a physical cause. Working out what the cause might be can be very difficult. However, it is reasonable to assume that if there is an underlying emotional cause then it must be quite serious if it is bad enough to cause pain. Here is a check-list of some of the less obvious causes of emotional distress in children:

- being teased or bullied
- difficulty with school work
- anxiety about relationships
- worries about parents' problems
- having a guilty secret
- feeling a failure.

Sometimes the cause of the stress has gone some time ago, but a child can become stuck with the pain which continues as a habit that may also be useful in getting sympathy and attention. If you think that this has happened, it is best to take little notice of the pain and expect your daughter to carry on with everyday life in spite of the discomfort, saying something like, 'Bad luck – can you help me over here for a minute?' as a distraction.

I think my child has developed a low self-esteem. What can I do about it?

Children with low self-esteem are quite easy to spot if you know what to look out for:

1. They avoid any task that is rather difficult or demanding.
2. They say they are worse than they really are.
3. They easily get into situations where they will fail.
4. They may even seem pleased to fail.
5. They accept criticism easily.
6. They react badly to praise.
7. They destroy anything good.

The more signs of low self-esteem there are, the more worrying it is because it can be quite difficult to get out of a vicious cycle of feeling a failure and getting it confirmed by failing all the time. Nevertheless it is possible to change how people feel about themselves, although it may take a long time. Even if you are doing everything right it will take at least three months.

There are three ways of helping children who feel a failure:

1. They must be protected from situations in which they are likely to fail. Remember, this may be difficult because they may deliberately seek out failure.
2. They need to experience success, so you will need to think of situations in which this can happen and make the most of any skills that they might have.
3. They need to be given extra praise and affection. This may be difficult because they may reject it, but it is important to press on regardless, even if your praise and affection are thrown back at you.

Children with a good self-esteem are so much better at coping with the rough and tumble of everyday life that it is worth while working very hard to make sure that your child has a positive self-image.

I am worried about my child's development, but don't know what to do about it

There are a number of different professionals who have

responsibility for checking on children's development. You will have met one or more of them already. They include the following people:

- general practitioner
- health visitor
- community health doctor
- paediatrician
- educational psychologist.

If you have already consulted some of the above people and would still like further advice, a referral to the local Child Development Centre would be a good idea. It is important to find someone whom you feel you can trust when discussing such an important matter, so keep looking until you find such a person.

There are many different voluntary organizations that deal with children whose development is either fast or slow. There is a great deal of variation round the country in how well these groups function. Perhaps the best thing is to go to your local library and go through the list of what is available locally and ask around the area to find out what other people think. Then try it and see what you think.

Further Reading

N. R. Butler and J. Golding (eds), *From Birth to Five* (Oxford: Pergamon Press, 1986).

M. Rutter (ed.), *Scientific Foundations of Developmental Psychiatry* (London: Heinemann, 1980).
An excellent reference book on the wider aspects of child development.

M. Rutter, J. Tizard and K. Whitmore (eds), *Education, Health and Behaviour* (London: Longmans, 1970; reprint New York: Robert Krieger Publishing, 1981).

A. Thomas and S. Chess, *Temperament and Development* (New York: Brunner/Mazel, 1977).

Index